P9-DEJ-208

Remembering James Agee

BOOKS BY DAVID MADDEN

FICTION

Bijou
Brothers in Confidence
Cassandra Singing
The Shadow Knows (short stories)
The Beautiful Greed

NONFICTION

Creative Choices (editor)
Studies in the Short Story (coeditor with Virgil Scott)
Nathanael West: The Cheaters and the Cheated (editor)
The Popular Culture Explosion: Experiencing Mass Media (coeditor with Ray B. Browne)
Rediscoveries (editor)
James M. Cain
American Dreams, American Nightmares (editor)
The Poetic Image in Six Genres
Tough Guy Writers of the Thirties (editor)
Proletarian Writers of the Thirties (editor)
Wright Morris

REMEMBERING
James Agee

Edited by David Madden

Louisiana State University Press

Baton Rouge

ISBN 0–8071–0086–2
Library of Congress Catalog Card Number 74–77326
Copyright © 1974 by Louisiana State University Press
All rights reserved
Manufactured in the United States of America

Designed by Dwight Agner. Set in 10/13 Simoncini Aster, printed on Warren's 1854 paper, and bound by Kingsport Press, Inc., Kingsport, Tennessee.

The editor gratefully acknowledges permission to reprint the following selections: Father James H. Flye, "An Article of Faith," *Harvard Advocate,* CV, No. 4; Robert Saudek, "J. R. Agee '32/ A Snapshot Album: 1928–1932," *Harvard Advocate,* CV, No. 4; Robert Fitzgerald, "A Memoir," from Robert Fitzgerald (ed.), *The Collected Short Prose of James Agee* (Houghton Mifflin Company, 1969); Walker Evans, "James Agee in 1936," from *Let Us Now Praise Famous Men* (Houghton Mifflin Company, 1960); Louis Kronenberger, "A Real Bohemian," from his *No Whippings, No Gold Watches,* copyright © 1965, 1970 by Louis Kronenberger, reprinted by permission of Little, Brown and Co., in association with the Atlantic Monthly Press; T. S. Matthews, "Agee at Time," *Harvard Advocate,* CV, No. 4, copyright © 1972 by T. S. Matthews; Dwight Macdonald, "Jim Agee, A Memoir," from his *Against the American Grain* (Random House, Inc., 1962); John Huston, "I See Him . . ." from his foreword to *Agee on Film,* Volume II (Grosset and Dunlap, Inc., 1960); and Whittaker Chambers, "Agee," from his *Cold Friday* (Random House, Inc., 1964).

Contents

Illustrations

All photographs are by Helen Levitt unless otherwise specified.

Remembering James Agee

On the Mountain with Agee

David Madden

IN OCTOBER, 1972, Saint Andrew's Episcopal School in Tennessee, held a commemorative gathering for the dedication of its James Agee Memorial Library. People who had either known Agee personally or who had been interested in or influenced by his work were invited to the school. The man who arranged this confluence of novelists, critics, scholars, clergymen, and students was David McDowell, Agee's biographer, custodian of the Agee Trust, and editor-publisher of *A Death in the Family.* Book review editors from the Nashville *Tennessean* and the Louisville *Courier-Journal* came, though none came from Knoxville. Scholars and writers came from universities in Texas, from Sewanee, Kenyon College, Vanderbilt, Harvard, Louisiana State University—though there were none from the University of Tennessee. Novelists whom McDowell had published came: Brainard Cheney, Frederick Manfred, Margaret Long, Madison Jones, Andrew Lytle, Warren Eyster, Bowen Ingram—few of whom ever met Agee in the flesh, but in whom his spirit now abides. Walker Percy came. Friends of Agee, Father Flye, eighty-eight that week, Dwight Macdonald, and Robert Fitzgerald came. And Mia Agee came, with her son John.

Skimming back through Agee's work before leaving Louisiana to participate in that week-long tribute to Agee at his boyhood school in Tennessee, I said to my wife: "You know, I really don't like Agee very much." I was reluctant to stop work on my own fiction to drive four hundred miles to struggle with ambivalent feelings about Agee. When *A Death in the Family* came out in 1957 and won the Pulitzer Prize, I was still a student, living a block away from Agee's childhood home, the locale of the novel. I was writing a novel set in Knoxville, which would be published a decade later by David McDowell. That Agee should be then the famous Knoxville writer I dreamed of becoming made me hellishly jealous. For if Dublin was Joyce's city, Knoxville was mine.

Over the years I had become convinced that the Agee legend, enhanced by publication of his letters to Father Flye, had inspired a sentimentality that beclouded his actual achievement as a writer. The romantic isn't-it-a-shame-he-died-before-he-could attitude was appealing, but I resisted it. When I first read Agee, especially *Let Us Now Praise Famous Men,* some passages struck me as precious, mannered, pompous. Though there were fine moments in *A Death in the Family,* Agee's poetry was pretentious and archaic. *The Morning Watch,* for me, was tedious and self-indulgent. I had to acknowledge that Agee was a superb movie critic and that his own movies, *The African Queen* and *The Night of the Hunter,* were wonderful. But his letters to Father Flye made me feel so queasy I couldn't read very far into them.

In that week of communion with Agee through his friends and admirers, and afterwards during months alone with Agee in his work, I was slowly converted to new attitudes about him. Many of us rediscovered Agee that week; but for me, as a writer and a teacher, something more than a rediscovery happened. A regenerative process began—a process that moved me to collect these previously published memoirs and to request new ones.

Trying to describe that experience I feel as Agee must have felt when he began *Famous Men:* "If I could do it, I'd do no writing at all here. It would be photographs; the rest would be fragments of cloth, bits of cotton, lumps of earth, records of speech, pieces of wood and iron, phials of odors." At Saint

Andrew's I touched no such talismanic objects inhabited by the spirits of those who had used them; rather I was taken by an aura, an atmosphere, a mood such as Agee caught in *The Morning Watch,* which is set at the school: "As if the whole air and sky were one mild supernal breath. . . ." This air became charged with an energy made manifest in what I must call signs, parallels to Agee's work, even symbols. Everything seemed runic to us. Like Good Friday in the novella, that week was one of those occasions when everything seems related, significant; coincidences were more strikingly coincidental than they normally are. A mystical note reverberated throughout that week-long ceremony of meditation that preceded the formal dedication of the library. Through his work and through the informal reminiscences of his friends, Agee's presence was most profoundly felt during that uncannily felicitous time on the mountain.

Watching the students at Saint Andrew's experience Agee through these men and women who had either known him or who felt that he had affected their lives or work, my own ambivalent feelings surfaced initially. The students, seventh- through twelfth-graders, had spent the entire semester with coordinated assignments in English classes, dealing with the entire range of Agee's work—short stories, a novella, a novel, poetry, personal journalism, movie criticism, television and movie scripts. Then for a full week, all classes were suspended to allow a massive immersion in Agee's work—discussion groups, movies, and panels conducted by the novelists, critics, and scholars. I sensed that some of the students were feeling as Rufus had felt in *A Death in the Family* when he was taken to visit his great-great-grandmother in the country: "It seemed to Rufus like a long walk over to the old woman because they were all moving so carefully and shyly; it was almost like church."

Like Agee in Alabama, we aliens risked being regarded as invaders, imposing a saint upon the students, forcing their participation, exacting their admiration and respect. I didn't want to contribute to a ritual in which students might be bored, bewildered, resentful, or even apathetic. When James Lee, editor of *Studies in the Novel,* disrupted the churchlike atmosphere with a blast at *Let Us Now Praise Famous Men,* I knew the students were as relieved as I was. As an Alabamian, Lee had resented Agee's romanticization of the suffering he knew as a country boy in the thirties. When the students applauded Lee's comments, I could only think that Agee himself would have appreciated such a clearing of the air.

When an English class met in the chemistry lab to discuss *A Death in the Family,* the teacher slumped between two Bunsen burners and confessed to being sick to death of talking about Agee. During the discussion that followed, the students and I began to share both our positive and negative feelings about Agee and his work. As I dealt with the various shifting literary and human contexts enacted at Saint Andrew's—with my own sometimes virulent objections and reservations—I realized that my responses to Agee's work were changing, my enthusiasm was growing.

Agee himself would, I think, have been entranced by the strategies some of the students used for defeating boredom, and by the grace with which they responded to particular moments in which insight, intellect, and emotion fused. I experienced some of those moments myself at a premier showing of a movie about Saint Andrew's, *School on the Mountain* by Charles Angermeyer, a young alumnus. In many ways, its images evoked several of Agee's works. In the film Father Flye reminisced about Agee and read from his writing. He also talked about teaching: "Not *I* against them, but they and I against the problem." Some students were beginning to respond to Agee as if he were such a teacher, and their "problem" was this week devoted to Agee. What an incredible teacher Agee would have been—a combination of Father Flye and Agee's other great teacher, I. A. Richards. In 1931, Agee had told Father Flye, "I am attracted to teaching almost enough to dread it . . . it would be very bad for me." He would have put all his intellect and emotion into it as he did with every job he ever had. In his writings, Agee did in fact presume to teach, and he was very conscious of the responsibilities.

This formal ceremony was now becoming not simply a structure in which normal breathing was difficult, but one in which a rarer kind of breathing had become possible. The already exhausted students endured the tedium of *All the Way Home*, the movie adaptation of *A Death in the Family*. Although I had been deeply moved when I first saw the film with my son, then Rufus' age, I disliked it intensely this time. Even so, I was profoundly affected by some of the parallels to my own life; I felt a compulsion to tell about those feelings in the discussion I led afterward. The movie theater scene was filmed in the Bijou, the setting of the novel I had put aside to come to Saint Andrew's. My father was living in the old L & N Hotel seen in the background as Rufus and his father walked home. John Cullum, who had acted in plays with me at the University of Tennessee, portrayed the agnostic uncle, Andrew.

Later, in my motel room, with the door open to let in the mountain mist, I returned to *Famous Men*. Now Agee as a man and a writer began to affect me as a reader and a writer. Agee's compulsion to transcend mere description moved him to devote four pages to overalls: "They are a map of a working man." In "new work-clothes a man has the shy and silly formal charm of a mail-order catalogue engraving." Agee sees "wild fugues and floods of grain" in old wood, "the patternings and constellations of the heads of driven nails . . . shadows strong as knives and India ink." I reread "Knoxville: Summer 1915"—"On the rough wet grass of the backyard my father and mother have spread quilts. We all lie there . . . and I too am lying there." Recalling a similar passage in *Famous Men*—Agee and Walker Evans lying on the porch of the Gudger house—I felt, in that midnight mountain air, that such a mood of felicity was what we all were beginning to create among ourselves, and that it was beginning to flow like a current between the increasingly faithful adults and the still somewhat skeptical students.

Just before the showing of Helen Levitt's and Agee's documentary, *The Quiet One,* Father Flye talked about Agee's religious life at Saint Andrew's. Father Flye is himself a quiet one; he hates microphones but knows he speaks softly and so uses his cupped hands as an amplifier. The restless kids stilled themselves in attentiveness. "Did Mr. Agee really believe his father's ghost was in the room?" one asked. The question transfixed Father Flye in contemplation; his eyes were wide in wonder, his mouth an O of awe; it seemed his very body was thinking. "What matters is not whether Agee himself believed in ghosts but that the people in the novel were convinced they felt the father's presence in the house." The tone of the students' feelings began to change now. I began to see that Agee, with lasting awe more than with clever paradox, regarded life and death as one unbroken process. More important than the effect of the father's death upon each member of the family was Agee's use of that death as an occasion to celebrate life in its everyday context of death.

Helen Levitt had sent us the original print of *The Quiet One,* with Agee's voice narrating. The movie opens with an Ageean dedication: "To all children who need help and to everyone who tries to help

them." Then, through the leaves, we see black boys running in the country. Hearing Agee's slow, quiet, natural, meditative voice with its slight Harvard accent just after Father Flye, the students became very still, respectful, and soon were deeply moved. We were beginning to reach out, less and less reluctantly, to touch Agee, as Rufus had reached for his father and Richard in *The Morning Watch* had reached for Christ.

Later there was an unscheduled showing of Agee's adaptation of Crane's *The Bride Comes to Yellow Sky*. In the opening scene, the town drunk stands in the window of the jail saying good-bye to the marshal. The marshal has given the drunk the jail key so that he can go over to the saloon for a drink and then lock himself back up. When the students in the audience suddenly realized that it was Jim Agee playing the drunk—moving, speaking, as if alive on the screen—they cheered. Seeing his own father for the first time in a movie, hearing him speak from the upper window of the jail as the town drunk, John Agee, Jim's nineteen-year-old son, seemed to experience an epiphany such as Richard had wanted. John's face, startlingly like his father's, lit by the reflections from the screen, had a similar effect, perhaps, on others in the audience.

John Agee had seemed rather aloof at first, a gangly young man striding slowly about the campus in a big grey hat he never removed, long hair bouncing on his shoulders. I was glad later to see John with Charles Angermeyer, the man who had filmed *School on the Mountain,* taking a long walk in the woods where Richard had walked after his morning watch. It seemed particularly appropriate that a young film-maker should be the first person to put John at ease in what must have been for him a claustrophobic atmosphere of adulation for a father he never knew.

The spirit of Agee had become embodied in us all, but it was most visible during the final panel discussion by men who had known him at different stages in his life or whose lives had been touched by his writings, many of whom have contributed to this collection of reminiscences: Father Flye, David McDowell, Dwight Macdonald, Robert Fitzgerald, Walker Percy, Andrew Lytle, and Robert Daniel. At first the panelists enacted a complex series of attitudes like the boys in *The Morning Watch* who undressed in front of each other to dive into the cold pond, but McDowell as moderator was so in tune with these men of very different sensibilities that he got from them the most remarkably amiable and productive public conversation among writers I ever expect to hear.

My own attitudes were affected by the comments of Walker Percy, himself a lover of movies, even bad ones. "I never knew Agee," he said. "I wish I had. I can only speak about his influence on me as a writer. I can best describe this influence as being technical. I do not think of Agee in connection with southern writers, but in connection with Englishmen and Irishmen, like Hopkins and Joyce—the early Joyce. His influence on me has been technical, simply, in the way that he crafts an English sentence, and uses poetic devices, metaphors, and sentence structure within a single paragraph."

And McDowell talked about Agee's approach to the *craft* of writing: "Agee welcomed criticism more than any writer I've ever known, and I've been working with them most of my life. He loved to read whatever he was working on to friends or to any group." To this Robert Fitzgerald eagerly added, "Jim was secure in that he knew that he was a decent writer. He could listen to the worst criticism, and he was generous and open about it. After all, what he was about was making something that was good. Whether or not this came about in an untouched singular effort, or with a few touches of assistance, doesn't matter at all. The important thing was to get it right and accurate with the words in the correct order. He was selfless in this area in many, many instances. What he wanted was good writing. If it was his, fine. If it was yours, equally fine—better, in fact."

Saint Andrew's became for me James Agee's cenotaph. The ceremony dedicating the library was short, hollow compared with, though indispensable to, the informal ceremonies that had by now become unforgettable. The Agee Memorial Library contains all of his works, memorabilia, photographs, the uncut *Omnibus* film about Lincoln. There are videotapes of guest novelists reading from Agee's work and of all the sessions of that week, with facilities for showing them. Signed books by friends and admirers are there. The library houses research material scholars will find unavailable elsewhere.

After leaving the mountain, I struggled to achieve some balance between skepticism and adulation. Reading and knowing Agee, many people have come to sense a saintly quality; but Agee must also have felt possessed of a devil sometimes. His obsession with original sin and the mortal sin of pride helps to explain his avocation of failure. The subtle dialectics of sin and guilt pervade his life and work. In *Famous Men* he apologizes for calling the tenant farmer's shack beautiful; then in a footnote he calls his apology the real sin. The very things before which they stand in awe, in fear or ecstasy, Agee's autobiographical characters Rufus and Richard feel they eventually betray. Somewhere in the tension between self-destructive guilt and creative overreaching, Agee expressed his finest moments of mental and emotional consciousness. He seemed to need some form of punishment simultaneous with joy—as when he lay on Gudger's mattress, vermin biting his flesh, his spirit perfectly attuned to the lives of the inhabitants.

Byronic in life and art, Agee was always keenly, often cripplingly, aware of the opposite possible truth to whatever he was passionately analyzing and advocating at the moment. Knowing the nature of things as they are, he looked at both sides. Like Scott Fitzgerald, Agee seemed to write out of a "dark night of the soul," where "it is always three o'clock in the morning, day after day." He seemed to struggle as actively and consciously as Fitzgerald to pass Fitzgerald's test of a first-rate intelligence: "the ability to hold two opposed ideas in the mind at the same time, and still retain the ability to function."

Although he was one of the most intellectual and analytical of modern American writers, Agee denied on every theoretical occasion that he was intellectualizing; he advocated constantly, in abstract terms, the necessity to rely mainly on the senses, instinct. Hypnotized by his own rhetoric in some passages of almost everything he wrote, Agee could make some irrevocably contradictory, even silly statements. His proclaimed antipathy to art was always expressed in the most artistic context and concepts and diction. He even tried to subvert whatever medium he was working in. "You should so far as possible forget that this is a book." But even as he jeeringly cautions his readers not to call his book a work of art, every page bears witness to his struggle to achieve nothing less. And a few pages after he laments his lack of imagination, he expresses a resentment of the "deifying of the imagination." His insights are forged in the crucible of the moment, and the medium of their expression ought, appropriately, to suffer the same time-fate; he wanted *Famous Men* printed on newsprint so that it would crumble in fifty years to dust.

Few writers have been as obsessed as Agee was with analyzing the difficulties of the creative process, and in the works of few writers has the suffering of the artist's vision been so much the subject of the work. On the Caedmon recording Agee recited a long list of possible jobs: "I simply have *got* to make a choice and—I can't." He describes the jobs in detail. "Right now I am in such a perplexity that my stomach is like a fist. I really cannot make up my mind to anything." One of the many jobs Agee described was writing the movie script about Paul Gauguin, in which the artist is presented "not as the criminal romantic, but as a man whose vocation was like a lure set out by God"; he would find after many years that "it was not the real thing even but only the lure and that all it was trying to teach him was to be as absolutely faithful to his own soul and his own being as he could, and that he find out the price of that as he went along." The script offers yet another autobiographical perspective on Agee.

Agee's achievement as an innovator and a forerunner in several media astonishes me. Along with Wright Morris, he was among the first imaginative writers to experiment seriously with phototext techniques. His work suggests the possibilities of imaginative nonfiction and anticipates, as McDowell has suggested, the personal journalism we find in Truman Capote and Norman Mailer in the sixties. Anticipating the current study of popular culture, he preached to the editors of the *Partisan Review* that "you learn as much out of corruption and confusion and more, than out of the best work that has ever been done." Agee was the first film reviewer to write of movies with personal commitment and a high seriousness. His descriptions of inanimate objects anticipate the experimental techniques of Robbe-Grillet's objectivism. I don't think he was deliberately innovative; rather his innovations seem to come out of a necessity implicit in the force of his temperament upon his material. Few American writers have been as responsive to media, high and low, as Agee; and that tendency attracts me to him because of my own compulsion to explore the possibilities of expression in all media.

Since the publication in 1957 of *A Death in the Family,* James Agee's reputation has remained strong among general readers and critics. All of his works are in print, most of them in paperback. His innovative approach to movie reviewing and personal journalism partly explain our interest in him today, twenty years after his death; respect for the artistry of his fiction remains high, and a reevaluation of his poetry seems imminent. But it is the legend of James Agee that has remained most consistently fascinating. He is with us now as an almost mythic presence.

With the mobility of the camera eye that so impressed him early in his life, Agee's omniscient vision moved among us on the mountain. We all seemed to move, that week, as if through "a ceremony of innocence"—no drowning as in Yeats's poem, but an emergence, as in *The Morning Watch.* Richard, too long submerged in his dive: *"Here I am!* his enchanted body sang." Many of us experienced a moment like Andrew's in *A Death in the Family:* "Andrew glanced quickly down upon a horned, bruised anvil; and laid his hand flat against the cold, wheemed iron; and it was as if its forehead gave his hand the stunning shadow of every blow it had ever received." So it was, for a moment, to touch Agee. Or to feel as Jay Follet's family did, that someone other than visible company is present in a room. With us, Agee finally achieved Richard's wish, to see mirrors face to face, endlessly reflecting each other. Agee lamented the inability of words to "communicate simultaneity with any immediacy." He exhorted the reader to collaborate imaginatively with him in *Let Us Now Praise Famous Men.* "Whence let me hope the whole of that landscape we shall essay to travel in is visible and may be known as there all at once." By the end of the week, all we knew and had felt about Agee, many of us knew and felt together in an intuitive simultaneity. Implicit in the letters of gratitude participants wrote to McDowell is a sense of communion. And through Agee, we all, as Macdonald testified, made lifelong friends. Like the multiconsciousness that resurrects Jay Follet's spirit even as his body is being buried, we achieved in our communion there on the mountain nothing less than a resurrection.

An Article of Faith

Father James H. Flye

IN 1905, on the Cumberland plateau in Middle Tennessee, two miles from Sewanee, some members of the Order of the Holy Cross, a monastic order of the Episcopal Church, started a little mission center, and for some young boys who were put under their care and a few others from the neighborhood, they provided teaching in school subjects and religion. From this developed Saint Andrew's School, which in a dozen years had come to have some seventy-five boarding boys and a few day students, with grades of instruction from primary up through high school.

It was a rural setting, a property of perhaps two hundred acres, some wooded, some under cultivation as a farm; a few dwellings, the school buildings, and the small monastery or priory where members of the order lived.

My connection with the place began in September, 1918, when I went there to teach in the school and be of assistance in some religious services and ministrations. My wife and I lived in a cottage on the school grounds. After the end of the school year, I stayed on there through the summer, as did some other persons of the staff and a few of the boys.

Mrs. Agee, whose home was in Knoxville, had friends at Saint Andrew's and in 1918, two years after the death of her husband, she with her two children had spent the summer there, living in one of the cottages. In 1919 they came again, and it was thus that I came to know them. James (or Rufus,

as he was then called, using his middle name which he came to dislike and later dropped entirely) was then in his tenth year, and Emma two years younger. And so began one of the most cherished and rewarding relationships of my life.

Many factors act as deterrents to rapport between individuals, but a difference of chronological age is not necessarily such, as Rufus and I soon discovered. Here was a friendly, intelligent boy, of active mind, fond of reading, with a good store of knowl-

edge and eager for more. There was no lack of things for us to talk about. He was interested in fossils and shells, knowing many by their scientific names which he used fluently and naturally. Then there was the subject of possible pets, and we discussed monkeys, ponies, elephants, rabbits, pigeons, and kangaroos, with citations from pet books and books of natural history. Then foreign countries, and Indian life, and Scout lore and woodscraft. He wanted a bow and arrows and we made a bow which he used some. Later he wanted a .22 rifle. It wasn't considered advisable to buy him one, but we borrowed one and did some target shooting. He wouldn't have thought of shooting at birds or rabbits or other living things.

But besides talk and doings such as just mentioned, there were real bonds between us in spirit, feelings, and instincts. He was very tender-hearted, touched to quick sympathy and pity at the sight or thought of suffering, human or other, and incapable of willingly causing it. He had a keen sense of humor and comedy, but was never comfortable with teasing or banter. He was by nature affectionate and trustful, with many endearing traits, and I felt deep tenderness and affection for him at this lovely age.

It may not be out of place here to include something told me years later by his mother of an incident in his childhood in Knoxville. "A friend of mine," she said, "was interested in a Settlement School out at the woolen mills. The women brought their children and they had to have people there in the nursery with them all day long while they worked in the mills. And she was taking Rufus in a little pony-cart or something. She had him with her to ride around to some of those places and she was telling him about those children. And Rufus said, 'Well, why do they have to stay in such a place? What are they there for?' She explained that they were very, very poor, which they were. And she said, 'You know, some of them don't even have shoes and stockings to wear.' And Rufus's eyes commenced to fill up and he was taking his shoes and stockings off then and there to give to whoever would need them. And that was like him, too. That continued to be like him, you know."

Some have felt James Agee saw in me something of a surrogate for his father, but I do not think this was the case. Our friendship and association and feeling toward each other were such, it seems to me, as we might equally well have had if his father had been living. As to the word *Father,* by the way, used by James Agee, that was simply standard usage at

Saint Andrew's in addressing or speaking of any priest.

With the passing of summer, I had assumed that Mrs. Agee would be returning to Knoxville, but she decided that as the cottage where they were living could still be had, she would stay on through the winter and have the children attend Saint Andrew's School. This arrangement was made and continued for the next four years, with visits in vacations at the home of Mrs. Agee's parents. In late February, 1924, when her father was not well, she left Saint Andrew's, and in 1924–1925 Rufus attended high school in Knoxville.

I was glad that our association was not to be broken off, but I could not help wondering how things would be with a boy like that in the regimen and surroundings to which he would have to adjust, with few of the boys of anything like his type or background. And he would undoubtedly be in trouble in the matter of some school rules and requirements; not by his intentionally breaking them, for he was not of defiant or uncooperative spirit, but because, though he meant well, he was absent-minded, forgetful of details, absorbed in what he was doing and not sufficiently conscious of time.

Life at Saint Andrew's School at that time was of rather plain and simple type. Most of the boys had very little money, and some really none. The charge for tuition and board was extremely low, and the school could not have carried on without the contributions sent in for its support. It was quite different from places modeled after the pattern of English schools. There was no system of rank and status within the student body, or between "old" and "new" boys, but general free choice of association and personal relations. Most of the boys were from rural or small-town background. The range in age was from a few very young boys to those in their upper teens, and three or four who after service in the First World War had come back to school for more education. The boys for the most part got on with each other very well, and the general spirit was friendly and pleasant. The boys took care of their own living quarters (with regular inspections) and each had some assigned job (changed every two weeks)—cleaning, waiting on table, pantry duty, or other inside or outside work about the place. As to scholastic aptitude and ability, the range was from boys who would never make any progress with "book learning" to those who would go to college and do well.

The religious commitment of Saint Andrew's was definite and strong. The head person there was the prior, appointed by and responsible to the father superior of the Order of the Holy Cross at West Park, New York, who would from time to time come for a visit. At the time of which we are writing, the prior was also headmaster of the school, and he taught one or two classes. The members of the order were not aloof but were friendly men and held in warm regard.

The aim and hope of the Holy Cross fathers at Saint Andrew's was to be of service in promoting Christian faith and practice in the form called Anglo-Catholic; a term designating the religious position of those in the Episcopal Church (or the Anglican Communion) who emphasize the organic historic continuity of the church and the teachings, rites and practice which bear witness to this. Some other places then or later with that same religious alignment would be the Church of the Advent and the Church of St. John the Evangelist in Boston and the monastery of the Cowley fathers in Cambridge.

In the school, attendance was required at daily chapel service and on Sundays at the sung mass and at evensong; grace was said at meals in the school dining room; and religious instruction was a required course in the curriculum. There was due observance of Lent, Holy Week, and other special seasons and days of the Christian year, and church boys were encouraged to go to Confession and Holy Communion. Many of the boys were acolytes and liked to take part thus in the church services. And each year would see a number of boys from other backgrounds coming into the church. It should be said here that what was emphasized in the religious teaching given at Saint Andrew's, whether in sermons or group instruction or personally, was not mere externals, though these had their place, but real Christian faith and devotion.

In this setting, then, James Agee spent the years of his school life from the age of ten to fourteen. For most of that time he had quarters in a dormitory, it being felt that this was better for him than living at home. Our friendship continued and developed, but not in any exclusive way. I was on very good terms with all the boys and we had many very pleasant associations; but with him there was a special fullness of understanding and communication. When he was eleven, just for fun, outside of school hours, I started him with French, in which he did well; and somewhat later, with another boy four years older who had had some French, we continued and read *Tartarin de Tarascon* which they greatly enjoyed. When he reached the ninth grade (high school) he was for the first time in one of my classes (English history), in which he was an excellent student.

After his return with his mother to Knoxville in the spring of 1923 I saw him occasionally; and in the summer of 1925 we spent two months in France and England, traveling mostly by bicycle. That fall he entered Phillips Exeter Academy, and during the next several years we met very seldom, but kept such contact as we might by writing. From 1941 to 1954 I took parish duty each summer in New York and we would see each other often.

When he first began to think of creative writing, or make any attempts at it in prose or verse, is not certain, but this does not seem to have been while he was at Saint Andrew's. On our trip abroad he spoke sometimes of wishing he could write something about things we had seen, but such feeling and such writing are not unusual. After getting to Exeter, however, that fall, his first letter to me spoke of his keen interest in writing and of his having written a story and two or three poems for publication in the *Monthly*.

A rich store of memories, impressions, and no doubt influences remained with James Agee from those years at Saint Andrew's: that Cumberland country of Middle Tennessee and its people; persons of all ages whom he had known—boys, teachers and others; and that school life in its various aspects and relations. I remember seeing pages of penciled jottings by him—single words, phrases, idioms, proper names—recalling persons, places, incidents, or experiences, unintelligible except to himself or perhaps someone in whom these might also stir recall. He made use of memories of this sort in his writings, and would have liked to use more. The scene of *The Morning Watch*—the dormitory, the Maundy Thursday Watch in relays through the night before the Blessed Sacrament—is unmistakably Saint Andrew's, and the originals of probably all the characters in that story would be easily recognizable by anyone familiar with that place in the early 1920s. He had deeply perceptive understanding toward his fellow human beings in their individual lives and would have liked to write more about them, and also to write some form of autobiography. *A Death in the Family* (which though called fiction is largely factual) shows what could be done with one episode in a life narrative.

Mrs. Agee was a devout and faithful church member of Anglo-Catholic convictions to whom the religious faith and practice at Saint Andrew's meant a great deal, and Rufus grew up well grounded in this teaching and practice and familiar with the language of the Bible and Book of Common Prayer.

He was an acolyte and used to serve often at the altar. In later years he felt unable to commit himself to full acceptance of some doctrinal statements of the church, but he had not abjured religion or Christian faith. He had a humble sense of wonder and reverence before the mysteries of the universe, of existence, of life, of human lives—a religious sense. There were many things about which he felt simply that he did not know, but he was not one of those who sit in the seat of the scornful. I remember his declaring his belief in "a divine or supernatural consciousness, power and love." As between the essentially religious and the non- or anti-religious, there is no doubt whatever in which category James Agee belongs. Read "Dedication" in the book of his poems.

He often had difficulties in regard to commitments, for he could not pledge himself to full support of or membership in an organization of any kind—political, social, economic, religious, or other—some of whose principles or policies he could not accept. He knew very well, however, the problems and difficulties of anyone considering this matter and what he should do.

He was truly humble, very conscious of weakness, shortcomings, and failures; a kind and loving person with great capacity for understanding and compassion, he will continue to speak through his writings. And to many there will be communicated thus the realization that here was one who had desires, hopes, uncertainties, moods, and emotions similar to theirs, one who would understand how they feel. For he did understand, and perhaps hoped that through something he had been able to put into writing some might come to feel more deeply the bond of our common humanity.

J. R. Agee '32
A Snapshot Album: 1928-1932

Robert Saudek

WHEN JIM DIED they took him to the tiny chapel of St. Luke's in Greenwich Village where his oldest friend, Father James Harold Flye, having finished the service, stepped to the head of Jim's coffin.

"It is not the custom of this church to eulogize its departed," he said. "I want to say only that anyone who ever met Rufus Agee will never forget him."

September, 1928. George Smith B-41

The door burst open and in strode the roommate—tall, shy, strong, long arms and legs, a small head, curly dark hair, a spring in his heels as he bounded past with a wicker country suitcase in one hand and an enormous, raw pine box on his shoulder. He turned his head suddenly, squinted his eyes in an apologetic smile, said softly, "Hello, Agee's my name," swept through to an empty bedroom and deposited his belongings, bounded back through the gabled, maroon-and-white study, murmured, "See you all later," waved an awkward farewell and didn't show up again for several days. Such was the magnetic field that had rushed through the room, that I didn't even think to introduce myself.

Now that I had at last seen him, heard him, and learned to pronounce his name, he was more of a stranger than before.

A week later Jim returned from his first morning of classes looking like a volcano. He went over to

the fireplace, turned and announced that he hated the place and hated a system that would seat "Agee" next to "Alsop" since that fat sonovabitch, not yet having bought himself a Latin textbook, picked up Agee's new book, opened it up and broke its spine, then clearing a great hock out of his throat, spat it on the open page. Jim swung his fist against the stucco wall above the fireplace with all his might, abrading his knuckles, and he felt so ashamed of this display that he then struck the bleeding fist against his own temple and leaned spent against the wall. He would not have said anything to Alsop; instead, he took it out on himself. He always did. That kind of eruption was awesome, for Jim was the most compassionate person and the least able to cope with insensitivity in others. The fact that he was a little older than some of us—and in experience was full grown—left me with the feeling that this was the way all the rest of us would react some day.

Jim did not especially love Harvard as he loved Exeter, but he did appreciate its people and its atmosphere of personal freedom. He could come and go at will. He could increasingly satisfy his need to feel secure with the styles, forms, and conceits of written English, and in a sense it would be the only kind of security he ever felt. But it was his comprehension of human behavior and a great fear of his own behavior that set him apart. For it was Jim who, coming back weak and sick from Stillman Infirmary to the Yard one midwinter's night, could smash his fist into the glass door of a moving streetcar on the Mt. Auburn Street line when the conductor closed the door in his face; who could rise at 4:30 on Sunday mornings to walk up the river and help the Cowley fathers serve communion at their Episcopal monastery; who would proudly struggle into white tie and tails in order to sing Bach in the Glee Club; who so adored Helen Hayes in *Coquette* that he saw it seven times in a week, who would spend a whole New York weekend in an all-night movie; who would mimic Lee and Grant at Appomattox ("Mah sword, Suh!" with an elaborate bow. "Drink to that!" replies General Grant sliding out of his chair onto the floor); who could sit up all night writing a poem or talking and smoking so that his fingers were stained to the color of a horse chestnut. The radius of his friendships extended beyond Harvard contemporaries, into the faculty, other colleagues, and out to his fellow workers in the summer wheat harvest. Jim listened carefully to each one of them.

September, 1930. Thayer 45

As junior year was about to start, a young man named Tom showed up—the kind of debonair outsider that Harvard always seems to attract: he was never enrolled as a student, yet he was completely at ease in the setting, alive with college gossip and stocked with faculty anecdotes. He would give a spell-binding account of a Broadway torch singer tangling with a big-name bootlegger; he dressed with casual correctness, spoke with the right accent, and in the long run became a very bothersome freeloader at mealtime and a tiresome schizophrenic, drunk by nine and knocking at your door by three A.M. in search of somebody to tell funny stories to.

Whole entries would conspire elaborately against Tom, but not Agee. Jim would answer the door, greet Tom with a low, "Hello, Tom," take him out to the entry's steps, and talk quietly until dawn, when Tom would either depart in peace or fall asleep in the stairwell. Whatever it was they found to talk about, Jim had a way of understanding it. He would frown, drop his head in staccato jerks and say quietly, "Sure, I know. . . . It's lousy. . . . Jesus knows it's lousy." Nothing could be more reassuring than when he went into that kind of litany.

By the time classes began we lost Tom in the reality of the business at hand, and so he sadly turned himself in to a mental institution for help, whence, for a few weeks, little mocking sparks flickered back to Cambridge. Most of us felt guilty for having done nothing, but Jim felt worst of all for not doing enough for Tom, whatever on earth that could possibly have been.

March, 1931. Thayer 45

In college one learns the significance of privacy. Anyone who, in high school, had been led to believe that privacy was antisocial if not unmanly, came to discover that in this college being by yourself was both respected and respectable.

In this discovery, Jim was a good preceptor for he thought and wrote in private; and when he was elated at his results he would ask quietly if I, or another friend, would mind listening to what he had just finished.

Once he wanted to talk about an idea loosely drawing on his interest in demonology. The idea was that a pair of adoring parents would have a beautiful baby who was perfect in every way but one: he was a cross between Don Juan and the Devil. Thus, as parents cooed over the cradle and sent out little blue-ribbon announcements, the dear little nipper would privately embarrass its mom by drawing blood like a vampire as it suckled, and by so titillating her in the process that she was driven close to madness in her attempts to put up a bold front, as it were. The precocity of her offspring was, to her, a total embarrassment—which would have delighted Jim for he believed in sentiment but deplored sentimentality.

I don't know where that poem is, but years later his long and marvelous poem, "John Carter," would state some such proposition without the mysticism, and with great wit:

Like Byron, I'll begin at the beginning.
Unlike that better bard, my lad's a new one,
Expert in charm, supremely so in sinning,
Nevertheless he differs from Don Juan
In ways enough to set your brain to spinning.

Then, with Chaucer's sense of weaving into wondrous tales the poet's own yarns, scruples, and distractions, Agee (stanzas later) reports on the progress of the devilish Leonard:

It flurried Leonard frightfully at times.
At night he thought of one thing and another,
Of sweet-fleshed maidens bred in palmier climes,
Also of Jesus, Hubert, and his mother.
So finally when he'd hoarded enough dimes,
He snuk to Boston . . . Well, I guess I'll smother
That little incident (which nearly threw him):
A friend has come, I want to read this to him.

The poem, wandering all over in time and space, finally treated events of the year 1935 as Agee writes resentfully of Tory England:

We wish you folks homesteading in the States
Would realize once for all that time and tide
Sooner or later make the earth our onion.
So won't you join the English Speaking Union?
. . . .
And thanks to British pluck and the
Almighty dollar,
We'll fit the whole world round to a Rhodes
collar.

But his desperate side, which Agee turned most often to the world, watching life corrode into death, x-rayed a lover's lips and saw a skull. Once during junior year Jim emerged from days and nights within himself and asked if he might read aloud an "Epithalamium" he had just completed. He first defined it as a poem to celebrate the joining of bride and bridegroom as they approach their marriage bed. Jim, who often formalized nature, explained that he thought of this marriage bed as the grave, and its canopy as the night sky; the bridegroom as destroyer; the bride as the destroyed; the bed as tombstone; the lovers as skeletons beneath their wedding raiments.

The private thoughts that had been working in his mind were transformed into words and rhythms written in a minor key, and his relief in beginning to read them aloud was very great.

Now day departs: upreared the darkness climbs
The breathless sky, leans wide above the fields,
And snows its silence round the muttering chimes:
The night is come that bride to bridegroom yields.

And eleven verses later he closed it:

Quiet, forever free from all alarms,
They lie where light is strengthless to descend.
The night is come, that hollows as it harms;
The night is come that day may never end.

January, 1932. Eliot G-52

As president of the *Advocate* Jim produced a parody issue, something I think this magazine had never done before, and it was a huge success. With his sense of containment within a form, Jim never let this caricature of *Time* magazine get out of hand and become a burlesque. The cover-picture had elegance: set within *Time*'s red-bordered cover was a fine photograph of a bronze Mercury poised lightly on one foot.

Jim had been so involved in writing, editing, picture-selecting, captioning, and layout that when the issue finally went to press, on a Saturday night, Jim went out to celebrate.

The next morning there was a note in the study asking me to wake him up as usual, since several of us had Sunday jobs in the First Church octet. Beside the note was a large, sealed manila envelope marked: "Metropolitan District Police, Defendant's Belongings."

I went in to wake him. His clothes were bloody, his sleeping face bruised, puffy, and cut.

On Saturday night Jim and his girl had gone out to Revere Beach for a winter's evening hike along the deserted boardwalk. Pretty much alone, they were singing, laughing, and drinking from a bottle of bootleg gin when two policemen came up and ordered them to pipe down. As the peace of that snow-swept beach was in no way being disturbed, Jim apparently reacted strongly enough that the two policemen, leaving Jim's girl behind, took him protesting, under each arm, lifted him in the air and gave him a bum's rush to precinct headquarters where he was booked, ceremoniously relieved of his belongings which were neatly sealed in an envelope, and then beaten up.

By dawn, Jim had managed to make bail through a Boston bail bond commissioner, picked up his envelope, called his girl, then struck out for Harvard Square. He felt no shame. He thought of himself as independent and responsible. He believed that the city of Revere should have wanted him to have a good time that night in their silent, snow-covered amusement park. That they did not want him to—that instead of protecting him they should have pummeled him—was beyond Jim's comprehension, and he was more confused than outraged by that brutal assault.

June, 1932. Class Day

As class poet, Jim had sat up all night on the last possible night, composing the class ode in pencil on coarse, unlined yellow sheets he purchased by the pound. It made the printer's at the last possible hour.

Class Day might not have concerned Jim but for the fact that as odist he was expected to appear in bachelor's gown with white frogs and the special cap marked by the muted crimson tassle of a Harvard class officeholder.

The coop being closed, Jim hustled a knee-length choir-robe from the First Church; and, from a Radcliffe senior, a girls'-style mortar board that sat primly on his head like a coronet with a long, red, Radcliffe tassle draped over his shoulders.

As the officers mounted the Sanders Theater stage, I think Jim really felt proud, for he was that day accepted into the elite band of classmates plucked from the ranks of football, polo, and the Banjo Club.

The ode was meant to be singable (though never sung) to the melody of "Fair Harvard," and Jim had tried desperately to commit it to memory and had pocketed his draft.

When his turn came, he sprang to the lectern and began to recite: "Now the winter is past and the storms of our youth,/We who gather to part in our power."

The lines rolled in that low, soft, somewhat monotone Tennessee cadence with its distinctive sibilance. But somewhere along the way he lost a word, and then a thought, and his eyes began to show terror, and he froze the audience of seniors with his helpless expression. Nobody laughed. Jim fished for a way into his gown to fetch the yellow sheets, but without success. Like a slow-motion film the pantomime seemed endless, until someone handed Jim the program which contained the printed text. He found his place, recovered and went on to the end:

And all wisdom we wring from our pain and desire
  On this field between devil and God,
Shall resolve to a white and unquenchable fire
  That shall cleanse the dark clay we have trod.

Jim went to commencement, but early that afternoon he was ready to hitchhike to New York to start his *Fortune* job. We stood among the half-packed trunks, textbooks, poems, unfinished stories, letters, term papers, prayer book, sheet music, photographs, and diplomas, and Jim and I shook hands, and we said so long and good luck and write. Four years were all over almost before they started. Then he lifted to his shoulder the raw pine box that held his phonograph, picked up his old wicker suitcase, and opened the door. I remember looking down from the window as he emerged five stories below and hiked across Eliot quadrangle with the heel-lifting stride he had brought with him four years before. The heavy pine box rested as lightly as a parrot on his shoulder.

He still seemed like Rufus or Jim, and we wanted to cling to that, but soon thereafter and forever, the world would know him only as James Agee.

Knoxville: Autumn, 1971

During October a visit to the University of Tennessee gave me a chance to find Jim's childhood neighborhood, which is the setting for *A Death in the Family* and some early short stories.

Like other Allegheny Mountain communities, Knoxville rises in steep waves of mined-out earth, so that every street seems to run uphill. Architecturally, his neighborhood is much the way he remembered it: "It was a little bit mixed sort of block, fairly solidly lower, middle class, with one or two juts apiece on either side of that." The frame houses still line up in white, gray or yellow. An occasional brick house of the twenties is soot-red. "The houses corresponded: middle-sized, gracefully fretted, wood houses built in the late nineties and early nineteen hundreds, with small front and side and more spacious back yards, and trees in the yards, and porches. There were fences around one or two of the houses."

There is an old, cast-iron picket fence next door to Rufus' front yard, but now its black spearheads are rusty and pock-marked and droop to left and right. The fence must once have been a low hurdle inviting small boys to clear it easily on the way home from school.

The sounds of a half-century ago are gone: the old West Knoxville Fire Hall, which was built down the block in 1906 for one horse-drawn pumper-engine, is gone, so the cobblestone racket of its fire horses and fire bells is gone.

The tracks of the Highland Avenue streetcar line that used to run in front of Rufus' house are interred in asphalt. "A streetcar raising its iron moan; stopping, belling and starting; stertorous; rousing and raising again its iron increasing moan and swimming its gold windows and straw seats on past and past and past . . . still fainter, fainting, lifting, lifts, faints forgone: forgotten."

Rufus spent his childhood in the second house from the corner, with a front porch that was garlanded with vines, at 1505 Highland Avenue in West Knoxville, Tennessee. That house and the corner house, 1503, were both razed in 1963. In their place has been erected the James Agee Apartments, three middlebrow stories of acne-colored brick, with outside galleries that stretch back from the street like cellblocks. A tiny pool, coffin-shaped, skinny and dry, sits beneath the cellblocks. "On the rough wet grass of the back yard my father and mother have spread quilts.

We all lie there, my mother, my father, my uncle, my aunt, and I too am lying there. First we were sitting up, then one of us lay down, and then we all lay down, on our stomachs, or on our sides, or on our backs, and they have kept on talking."

The alley that runs behind the houses of the 1500 block, and was Rufus' alley, gave access to all the backyards, which are still wide and deep but turned to weeds. The trees are out of hand and choking with nondescript vines. The back fences along the alley have been replaced, but their heavy old iron bolts remain. The neighbors still hang their wash out back from clotheslines strung between T-poles. A few small barns, windowless, paintless, and exhausted, have been padlocked for years.

The backyard of 1505 is no longer rough, wet grass. It is concrete clear out to the alley, and beyond it is a tenants' parking lot for the James Agee Apartments. "Who shall ever tell the sorrow of being on this earth, lying, on quilts, on the grass, in a summer evening, among the sounds of night."

The apartments, like the older dwellings along Highland Avenue, are occupied by students of the neighboring University of Tennessee.

A pleasant young man emerged and began to climb into his green VW.

Q: Do you know the name James Agee?
A: I don't, but there's a directory of everybody who lives in the building right inside.
Q: Well, James Agee has been dead for some years.
A: O, I'm sorry.

I knocked at the door of 1507, a gray frame house of the vintage, and a very frail old lady answered the door.

A: Yes, I remember when the Agee family lived there . . . I think I do . . . I've been here quite awhile.
Q: Since the twenties?
A: (Pause) I'd have to look it up. I know I've lived here quite awhile.

"There were few good friends among the grown people, and they were not poor enough for the other sort of intimate acquaintance."

Jim's memory of Highland Avenue, Forest, 15th Street, the nearby viaduct and the L & N Depot below it, was long and vivid. But living inhabitants did not remember. There was no evidence of curiosity about the black-and-white sign out front, JAMES AGEE APARTMENTS. TOWN AND COUNTRY CONSTRUCTION CO. AGENTS. PHONE 572-2083. Two English department professors at the university had no notion where it was that Agee had lived and written of, although they were sitting three blocks away from that sign. It seemed odd. Yet we, as students, had never given a thought to who either Thayer or George Smith was. That's the way it is.

Around three o'clock a boy about eight years old came walking along the old, iron fence. He was carrying home from school a folded sling, pasted with paper handles and filled with several sheets of lined tablet paper covered with the painful handwriting of a beginner. That is the closest I came to a living memory of Jim.

A Memoir

Robert Fitzgerald

THE OFFICE BUILDING where we worked presented on the ground floor one of the first of those showrooms, enclosed in convex, nonreflecting plate glass, in which a new automobile revolved slowly on a turntable. On Sunday a vacant stillness overcame this exhibition. The building bore the same name as the automobile. It had been erected in the late twenties as a monument to the car, the engineer, and the company, and for a time it held the altitude record until the Empire State Building went higher. It terminated aloft in a glittering spearpoint of metal sheathing. From the fifty-second and fiftieth floors where Agee and I, respectively, had offices, you looked down on the narrow cleft of Lexington Avenue and across at the Grand Central Building, or you looked north or south over the city or across the East River toward Queens. As a boom-time skyscraper it had more generous stories than later structures of the kind—higher ceilings, an airier interior. Office doors were frosted in the old-fashioned way prevalent when natural daylight still had value with designers. In a high wind at our altitude you could feel the sway of the building, a calculated yielding of structural steel. Thus contact of a sort was maintained with weather and the physical world. In our relationship to this building there were moments of great simplicity, moments when we felt like tearing it down with our bare hands. We would have had to work our way from interior partitions to plaster shell to exterior facing, ripping it away, girder after girder, until the whole thing made rubble and jackstraws in 43rd Street. Jim was vivid in this mood, being very powerful and long boned, with long strong hands and fingers, and having in him likewise great powers of visualization and haptic imagination, so that you could almost hear the building cracking up under his grip.

He was visited on at least one occasion by a fantasy of shooting our employer. This was no less knowingly histrionic and hyperbolic than the other. Our employer, the Founder, was a poker-faced, strong man with a dented nose, well-modeled lips, and distant gray-blue eyes under bushy brows; from his boyhood in China he retained something, a trace of facial mannerism, that suggested the Oriental. His family name was a New England and rather a seafaring name; you can find it on slate headstones in the burial grounds of New Bedford and Nantucket and Martha's Vineyard. These headstones in the middle years of the last century were fitted with tintypes of the dead as living reminders on the spot of what form they were to reassume on the Last Day, provided that the day should occur before the tintypes utterly faded, as now seems not altogether unlikely. The Founder had that seacoast somewhere in him behind his mask, and he had a Yankee voice rather abrupt and twangy, undeterred by an occasional stammer. A Bones man at Yale, a driving man and civilized as well, quick and quizzical, interested and shrewd, he had a fast sure script on memoranda and as much ability as anyone in the place. He had nothing to fear from the likes of us. Jim imagined himself laying the barrel of the pistol at chest level on the Founder's desk and making a great bang. I imagine he imagined himself assuming the memorable look of the avenger whom John Ford photographed behind a blazing pistol in *The Informer*. It is conceivable that the Founder on occasion, and after his own fashion, returned the compliment.

The period I am thinking of covers 1936 and 1937, but now let me narrow it to late spring or early summer of 1936. Roosevelt was about to run for a second term against Alf Landon, and in Spain we were soon to understand that a legitimate republic had been attacked by a military and Fascist uprising. One day Jim appeared in my office unusually tall and quiet and swallowing with excitement (did I have a moment?) to tell me something in confidence. It appeared very likely, though not yet dead sure, that they were going to let him go out on a story, a story of tenant farming in the Deep South, and even that they would let him have as his photographer the only one in the world really fit for the job: Walker Evans. It was pretty well beyond anything he had hoped for from *Fortune*. He was stunned, exalted, scared clean through, and felt like impregnating every woman on the fifty-second floor. So we went over to a bar on Third Avenue. Here I heard, not really for the first time and certainly not for the last, a good deal of what might be called the theory of *Let Us Now Praise Famous Men,* a book that was conceived that day, occupied him for the next three years, and is the center piece in the life and writing of my friend. It may occur to you that if he had not been employed in our building and by our employer (though upon both at times he would gladly have attracted besides his own the wrath of God), he would never have had the opportunity of writing it. That is true; and it is also true that if he had not been so employed the challenge and the necessity of writing it might never have pressed upon him so gravely as for some years to displace motives for writing, other ends to be achieved by writing, including those of which the present book is a reminder.*

2

The native ground and landscape of his work, of his memory, was Knoxville and the Cumberland Plateau, but his professional or vocational school was one that for a couple of years I shared. You entered it from shabby Cambridge by brick portals on which were

* All references to "the book" refer to the *Collected Short Prose of James Agee.*

carven stone tablets showing an open book and the word *veritas,* a word—not that we paid it then the slightest attention—destined to haunt us like a Fury. The time I am thinking of now is February of 1930 in the Yard of that college where the stripped elms barely shadowed the colonial brickwork, and planks on the paths bore our feet amid clotted snow. On a Wednesday afternoon in the dust of a classroom I became sharply aware for the first time of Mr. Agee, pronounced quickly *Aygee.* We had been asked each to prepare a lyric for reading aloud. The figure in the front row on my right, looming and brooding and clutching his book, his voice very low, almost inaudible, but deliberate and distinct, as though ground fine by great interior pressure, went through that poem of Donne's that has the line *A bracelet of bright hair about the bone.* It was clear that the brainy and great versing moved him as he read. So here, in the front row, were shyness and power and imagination, and here, moreover, was an edge of assertion, very soft, in the choice and reading of this poem, because the instructor for whom he was reading did not belong to the new School of Donne.

After this, Agee and I would sometimes have a Lucky together and talk for a few minutes outside Seaver Hall in the bitter or sweet New England weather. Seniority was his, then and for that matter forever, since he was a year older and a class ahead. He lived in the Yard and we had no friends in common. Older, darker, larger than I, a rangy boy, alert and gentle, but sardonic, with something of the frontiersman or hillman about him—a hard guy in more than the fashion of the time—wearing always a man's clothes, a dark suit and vest, old and uncared for, but clothes. His manner, too, was undergraduate with discrimination. He was reading Virgil that year under a professor whose middle initial had drawn down upon him the name of Pea Green William; Agee grimly referred to him strictly as Green. In the Seaver classroom with a handful of others we gave our attention to English metrics as expounded by our instructor, the Boylston Professor, who had set his face against Eliot and Pound. Faintly graying, faintly blurred, boyish and cheerful, mannerly and mild, he turned back to us each week our weekly sets of verses with marginal scrawls both respectful and pertinent. He was also good at reading aloud. Our metrical sense was educated by such things as the hovering beat of "Hark All You Ladies," and we heard the heroic couplet doomed by Romantic orchestration in "Whether on Ida's Shady Brow."

Far away from college, in the realm where great things could happen, great things had in fact happened that year: works of imagination and art in newly printed books, and these we pored and rejoiced and smarted over: *A Farewell to Arms,* most cleanly written of elegies to love in war, in the Great War whose shallow helmets, goggled masks and khaki puttees were familiar to our boyhood; *Look Homeward, Angel,* the only work by an American that could stand with *A Portrait of the Artist as a Young Man;* and *The Innocent Voyage,* from which we learned a new style of conceiving childhood. Agee and I were very fond of these books. We were also devoted to Ring Lardner and to all the Joyce that we knew. But "The Waste Land," which had made my foundations shift, had not affected him in the same way, nor did "Ash Wednesday" seem to him as uncanny and *cantabile* and beyond literature as it did to me. Here we diverged, and would remain divided in some degree, as he desired in poetry something both more and less than I did, who chiefly wanted it to be hair-raising.

In the *Harvard Advocate* that year there were poems by J. R. Agee, but to my intolerant eye they seemed turgid and technically flawed. I did not see until several years later the highly mannered and rather beautiful "Epithalamium" that he wrote in the spring. "Ann Garner" was a more complicated matter. This longish poem appeared in the quarterly, *Hound & Horn,* still known that year by the subtitle, *A Har-*

vard Miscellany, and edited by the princely Lincoln Kirstein, then in his last year as an undergraduate. Kirstein had known James Rufus Agee as a new boy at Exeter four or five years before, and there is a passage on Jim in his book, *Poems of a Pfc.,* finally published in 1964. "Ann Garner" had been written, in fact, while Jim was still at Exeter in 1928. Boys in prep school do not often write anything so sustained, and it is clear from one of Jim's letters what an effort it had been. In the first year of our friendship it impressed me more than any of his other verse for the ambition of the attempt at narrative with variations, not really like Jeffers but reaching like him toward myth, a vision of elemental life in the American earth.

What brought me fully awake to Agee as a writer was not this poem, callow even in its power, but a short story in the April *Advocate.* Two boys hunting with a BB gun in the outskirts of Knoxville got some infant robins out of a nest and decided they must be "put out of their misery," so while the mother bird flew shrill and helpless overhead they did the deed with stones. In puzzlement, in awe, in fascination, in boastful excitement—in shame, in revulsion. The younger boy threw up; the boys went home. That was about all, but the writer fully realized and commanded his little event. When I reread this story after thirty-three years I saw that he had put into it some of the skills and passions of his life: sympathy with innocent living nature, and love of it; understanding of congested stupidity and cruelty, and hatred of it; a stethoscopic ear for mutations of feeling; an ironic ear for idiom; a descriptive gift. No other contributor to the *Advocate* that year (in what other year?) wrote with ease, and repeatedly, prose like this: "The birds were very young. A mildew fuzz covered their heads and backs, along their wings lay little white spikes, like hair-fine fishbones. Through the membrane globing their monstrous bellies the children could see a mass of oystery colours, throbbing faintly. The birds kicked, and gaped, and clenched their wings." Significantly, too, the story intimated a pained interest in the relation between the actuality of birds and boys—kicking and gaping—and the American institution of "Church" or weekly Christian observance. The two hunters, parting uneasily after their crime, agreed to meet at Sunday school.

3

By simply descending a flight of steps and pushing through a turnstile for a nickel you could leave the university behind and set off for the big-city mystery of Boston, where wine in coffee cups could be drunk at the Olympia or *arak* at the Ararat on Atlantic Avenue; then other adventures would follow. If the Yard was our dooryard, Boston and neighborhood were the backyard we explored, and Jim later wrote a short catalogue of attractions that he liked:

> Window table in Tremont St. Childs, brilliant Sunday midmorning; the New England Boxing Tournament, for steady unsparing (if unskillful) ferocity; Boston Common with an actor and hangover and peanuts and pigeons, midafternoon; the Common on a rainy afternoon or night; on a snowy night; on a Sailor's night; the Fenway at about dusk, fair weather; for good movie stuff: the Arlington Theatre and lampposts from just beyond the level bridge; the debouchement of the Forest Hills subway . . . Revere Beach in midwinter, for sea sounds and pure ghoulishness; East Boston for swell houses, stunted trees struck through with mordant street lamps, and general dilapidation; the Arnold Arboretum in October or May; up the Charles at midnight, down at dawn; the fishboats unloading before dawn.

We lacked neither opportunity nor time for excursions like these and for a good deal of what we had to concede was Young Love. As for the university, it could be contented with a few classes a week and a few sleepless nights before exams. Considering human bondage in general and the demands of any other mode of life, it is remarkable that Agee and I both talked of breaking for freedom from this one, but we did, and he even had a plan of bumming to the Coast that spring on the chance of getting a movie job. If he had, the American cinema might have felt his impact twenty years before it took place. I reconcile myself to things having turned out as they did. He waited until summer and went west to work as a harvest hand and day laborer in Oklahoma, Kansas, and Nebraska.

Jim had been briefly in England and France in the summer of his sixteenth year, on a bicycle trip with his boyhood and lifelong friend, Father James Flye. Although he never returned to Europe, he had absorbed enough to sharpen his eye and ear for his own country. It can be said of him that he was American to the marrow, in every obvious way and in some not so obvious, not at all inconsistent with the kind of interest that some years later kept us both up until three in the morning looking through drawings by Cocteau, or some years later still enabled him to correct for me a mistranslation of Rimbaud. He took Patrick Henry's alternatives very seriously. Deep in him there was a streak of Whitman, including a fondness for the barbaric yawp, and a streak of Twain, the riverman and Romantic democrat. What being an American meant for an imaginative writer was very much on his mind. His summer wandering fell in, so to speak, with his plans.

Two short stories written out of his working summers appeared in the next year's *Advocate* and are reprinted in this book. They are the last fiction Jim published as a young man, the last he would publish until *The Morning Watch* in 1950. In both stories you may feel the satisfaction of the narrator in being disencumbered of his baggage, intellectual or cultural, urban and familar and social, and enabled to focus on the naked adventure at hand. The adventure in each case partly happened and was partly made up; the stories are pure fiction in the usual way of pure fiction, as much so as stories by Hemingway, their godfather. My point is that to conceive and feel them on his skin he had deprived himself of all the distraction that he liked—company, music, movies, and books—and had lived in lean poverty like a lens. To write them, and almost everything else that he had to work on for any length of time, he took on destitution by removing himself from class-bells, Thayer Hall, and his roommates, and holing up in the *Advocate* office for days and nights until the job was done. Advocate House at that time was a small frame building up an alley, containing a few tables and chairs and an old leather-covered couch, all pleasantly filthy; and there were, of course, places round about where you could get coffee and hamburgers or western sandwiches at any hour of the night. A boardinghouse bedroom or an empty boxcar might have been still better.

Did he ever draw any conclusions from all this? He certainly did. He never forgot what it meant to him to be on the bum, and he managed it or something like it when he could. His talent for accumulating baggage of all the kinds I have mentioned was very great, as it was very endearing, and he spent much of his life trying to clear elbowroom for himself amid the clutter. But on the question as to whether he had any business coming back to college that year, his third and my second, the answer is Yes, and the best reason was Ivor Armstrong Richards.

In the second semester, on his way back to Magdalene, Cambridge, from a lectureship at Tsing Hua University in Peking, Richards paused at Harvard and gave two courses, one on modern English literature and the other carrying on those experiments in the actual effects of poetry that he had begun at Cambridge and had written up in his book, *Practical Criticism* (1929). Jim and I attended both courses and found ourselves at full stretch. Though he appeared shy and donnish, Richards was in fact intrepid and visionary beyond anyone then teaching literature at Harvard; when he talked about our papers he sometimes gave me the impression that he had spent the night thinking out what he would say in the morning. By pure analysis he used to create an effect like that produced by turning up an old-fashioned kerosene lamp, and he himself would be so warmed and illuminated that he would turn into a spellbinder, gently holding sway, fixing with his glinting gray eyes first one quarter and then another of the lecture room. When he spoke of the splendors of Henry James's style or of Conrad facing the storm of the universe, we felt that he was their companion and ours in the enterprise of art.

Richards' exacting lucidity and Jim's interest in the "Metaphysicals" are reflected in a poem in octosyllabics called "The Truce," printed in the *Advocate* for May, 1931, the first poem of Jim Agee's that seemed to me as fully disciplined and professional as his prose. I not only admired but envied it and tried to do as well. The image of the facing mirrors fascinated him and made its last appearance in his work twenty years later, in *The Morning Watch* and in his commentary for the film, *The Quiet One.* There is an echo in "The Truce," as there is also in one of the sonnets, of a great choral passage ("Behold All Flesh Is As the Grass") in the Brahms *Requiem,* which he sang that spring in the Harvard Glee Club; the surging and falling theme stayed in our heads for years.

Along with his stories, "The Truce" would be evidence enough—though there is explicit evidence in one of his letters—that in the spring of 1931 Jim held the English poetic tradition and the American scene in a kind of equilibrium under the spell of Richards, and lived at a higher pitch, but at the same time more at ease with his own powers, than in any other college year. He was elected president of the *Advocate* and thus became the remote Harvard equivalent of a big man on campus. We still saw one another rarely aside from class meetings, but had now one or two friends in common including Kirstein and a superb girl at Radcliffe, a dark-eyed delicately scornful being who troubled him before she troubled me; I can still see his grin of commiseration and tribute.

4

In the world at large where the beautiful books had happened, something else had begun to happen that in the next few years fixed the channel of Jim Agee's life. I was in England in 1931–1932 and saw nothing of him that year, when he got his degree, nor in the next year when I was back at Harvard to get mine. What gradually swam over everyone in the meantime was an ominous and astringent shadow already named by one cold intellect as the economic consequences of the peace. Worse evils and terrors were coming, but at the time this one seemed bad enough, simple as it was. People had less and less money and less and less choice of how to earn it, if they could earn any at all. Under a reasonable dispensation a man who had proved himself a born writer before he left the university could go ahead in that profession, but this did not seem to be the case in the United States in 1932. Neither in Boston nor New York nor elsewhere did there appear any livelihood appropriate for a brilliant president of the *Harvard Advocate,* nor any mode of life resembling that freedom of research that I have sketched as ours at Harvard. In the shrunken market the services of an original artist were not in demand. Hart Crane and Vachel Lindsay took their lives that spring. Great gifts always set their possessors apart, but not necessarily apart from any chance to exercise them; this gift at that time pretty well did. If a freshman in 1929 could feel confined by the university, in 1932 it seemed a confinement all too desirable by contrast with what lay ahead—either work of the limited kinds that worried people would pay for, or bumming in earnest, winter-bumming, so to say. Agee thankfully took the first job he could get and joined the staff of *Fortune* a month after graduation.

During the next winter, back in Cambridge, where my Senior English tutor was studying *Das Kapital* and referred to capitalist society as a sick cat, we heard of

Jim working at night in a skyscraper with a phonograph going full blast. Thus a writer of fiction and verse became a shop-member on a magazine dedicated by the Founder to American business, considered as the heart of the American scene. It is odd, and, I think, suspicious that even at that point in the Great Depression Jim did not live for a while on his family and take the summer to look around. Dwight Macdonald, then on the staff of *Fortune,* had been in correspondence with Jim for a year or two and had bespoken a job for him on the strength of his writing—which incidentally included a parody of *Time,* done as one entire issue of the *Advocate.* The man who was then managing editor of *Fortune* was clever enough to recognize in Agee abilities that *Fortune* would be lucky to employ, and he would have had it in him to make Jim think he might lose the job if he did not take it at once. I do not know, however, that this occurred. What else Jim could have done I don't know either; but again at this time there was the alternative of Hollywood, and there might have been other jobs, like that of forest ranger, which would have given him a healthy life and a living and left his writing alone. Now and again during the next few years he would wonder about things like that.

At all events, he hadn't been on *Fortune* three months before he applied for a Guggenheim Fellowship, in October, 1932. Nothing came of this application, as nothing came of another one five years later. In the 1932 application (of which he kept a carbon copy among his papers) he proposed as his chief labor the continuation of a long satirical poem, *John Carter,* which he had begun at Harvard, and said he would also perhaps finish a long short story containing a "verse passacaglia." The title of the story was to be "Let Us Now Praise Famous Men"; I never saw and have not recovered his draft of it. For opinions of his previous writing he referred the judging committee to Myron Williams, an English teacher at Exeter, Conrad Aiken, and I. A. Richards. For opinions of *John Carter* he referred them to Archibald MacLeish, Stephen Vincent Benét, Robert Hillyer, Theodore Spencer, and Bernard DeVoto. Phelps Putnam, he said, would also be willing to give an opinion. If awarded a fellowship he would work mainly on the poem, "which shall attempt a diversified and comprehensive reflection and appraisal of contemporary American civilization and which ultimately, it is hoped, will hold water as an 'Anatomy of Evil.' " He would work on it "as long as the money held out" and he thought he could make it last at least two years. "I don't think I would spend much time about any university," he said; "I expect I would live in France, in some town both cheap and within reach of Paris." It is a fair inference from this that in October, 1932, he did not yet know that he would marry Olivia Saunders in the following January. Both in October and January he must have considered that he had a good chance of a Guggenheim. On his record he was justified in thinking so. Yet in the last sentence of his "project" for *John Carter* his offhand honesty about the prospect of never finishing it may have handed the Guggenheim committee a reason for turning him down.

The two long sections that he got written, with some unplaced fragments, have been printed in *The Collected Poems of James Agee.* His hero, never developed beyond conception in the poem as it stands, would have owed something not only to Byron's Don Juan but, I think, to the Nihilist superman Stavrogin in *The Possessed* of Dostoevsky, a novel we were studying with Richards in the spring of 1931—greatly to the increase of hyperconsciousness in us both. Jim's fairly savage examination of certain Episcopalian attitudes and décor—and even more, the sheer amount of this—indicates quite adequately how "Church" and "organized religion" in relation to awe and vision, bothered his mind. Another value, almost another faith, emerges in the profound respect (as well as disrespect) accorded to the happy completion of love. When Jim spoke of "joy" he most often meant this, or meant this as his criterion.

5

Moderate ambitions may be the thing for some people at some ages, but they were not for James Agee, and certainly not at twenty-three. To make "a complete appraisal of contemporary civilization," no less, was what he hoped to do with his long poem. Now the Founder, Henry Luce, with his magazines, actually held a quite similar ambition, and this accounts for the mixture of attraction and repulsion in Agee's feeling for his job. Attraction because *Fortune* took the world for its province, and because the standard of workmanship on the magazine was high. Also because economic reality, the magazine's primary field, appeared grim and large in everyone's life at that time, and because by courtesy of *Fortune* the world lay open to its editors and they were made free of anything that in fact or art or thought had bearing on their work. Repulsion because that freedom in truth was so qualified, because the ponderous and technically classy magazine identified itself from the start, and so compromised itself (not dishonestly, but by the nature of things), with one face of the civilization it meant to appraise; whatever it might incidentally value, it was concerned with power and practical intelligence, not with the adventurous, the beautiful and the profound—words we avoided in those days but for which referents nonetheless existed. At heart Agee knew his vocation to be in mortal competition, if I may put it so, with the Founder's enterprise. For *Fortune* to enlist Agee was like Germany enlisting France.

Nevertheless he had now three uninterrupted years of it. One blessing was the presence on *Fortune* of Archibald MacLeish, a Yaleman like the Founder and one of the original editors, but also a fine artist who knew Jim for another, respected him and helped him.

MacLeish in 1932 was forty and had published his big poem, *Conquistador*. Being experienced and distinguished, he could pick the subjects that appealed to him, and being a clearheaded lawyer-turned-poet, he wrote both well and efficiently. His efficiency was a byword on *Fortune*. Requiring all research material on cards in orderly sequence, he merely flipped through his cards and wrote in longhand until five o'clock, when he left the office. Often enough other people, including Jim, would be there most of the night.

I had a brief glimpse of the scene when I got to New York in the summer of 1933. The city lay weary and frowsy in a stench of Depression through which I walked for many days, many miles up and down town, answering ads, seeing doubtful men in dusty offices, looking for a job. MacLeish got me an interview with a rather knifelike *Fortune* editor who read what writing I had to show and clearly sized me up as a second but possibly even more difficult Agee, where one was already enough. Staring out of the window reflectively at Long Island he told me in fact that the Founder had taken a good deal from Agee, allowing for Agee's talent, but that there were limits. Back in MacLeish's office I waited while he, the old backfield man, warm and charming as ever, called up Jim. So Jim came in and we poets talked. One subject was the current plight of Kenneth Patchen, a poet dogged by misfortune. Archie also mentioned Hart Crane, whom he had once persuaded *Fortune* to take on for a trial. Hart had been completely unable to do it. It did not cross my mind that this had any relevance to me. I felt elated over my visit, and Jim took me home to dinner.

The basement apartment on Perry Street had a backyard where grew an ailanthus tree, and there under the slim leaves we sat until dark, he and Via and I, drinking I don't remember what but I imagine Manhattans, a fashion of the period. After dinner we went to the piano and sang some of the Brahms

Requiem. Then he got out his manuscripts, read from *John Carter,* and read a new poem, a beauty, "Theme with Variations" (later he called it "Night Piece"). *Fortune,* I suppose at MacLeish's suggestion, had assigned him an article on the Tennessee Valley Authority, and in the course of preparing it he had gone back that summer to the countryside of his boyhood: hence, I think, this poem. In that evening's dusk and lamplight neither of us had any doubt that we shared a vocation and would pursue it, come what might. We were to have a good many evenings like it during the next three years while that particular *modus vivendi* lasted for Jim Agee as office worker and husband.

Jim must have thought *Fortune* would have me (*Time,* instead, had me, but not until February of 1936), because at the end of August when I was temporarily out of town I had a letter from him that concluded: "I'm wondering what you'll think of a job on *Fortune,* if you take it. It varies with me from a sort of hard, masochistic liking without enthusiasm or trust, to direct nausea at the sight of this symbol $ and this % and this *biggest* and this some blank billion. At times I'd as soon work on *Babies Just Babies.* But in the long run I suspect the fault, dear *Fortune,* is in me: that I hate any job on earth, as a job and hindrance and semisuicide."

His TVA article appeared in *Fortune* for October. It opened:

> The Tennessee River system begins on the worn magnificent crests of the southern Appalachians, among the earth's older mountains, and the Tennessee River shapes its valley into the form of a boomerang, bowing to its sweep through seven states. Near Knoxville the streams still fresh from the mountains are linked and thence the master stream spreads the valley most richly southward, swims past Chattanooga and bends down into Alabama to roar like blown smoke through the flood-gates of Wilson Dam, to slide becalmed along the crop-cleansed fields of Shiloh, to march due north across the high diminished

plains of Tennessee and through Kentucky spreading marshes toward the valley's end where, finally, at the toes of Paducah, in one wide glassy golden swarm the water stoops forward and continuously dies into the Ohio.

Soon after this Luce called him in and told him that he had written one of the best things ever printed in *Fortune*. It was characteristic of the Founder to acknowledge this; it was also characteristic of him to indicate, as Agee's reward, the opportunity to write a number of straight "business stories" whereby to strengthen his supposed weak side. The first of these concerned the Steel Rail, and according to Dwight Macdonald, the Founder himself buckled down to coach Agee in how to write good hard sense about the steel business. A story later got around that the Founder for a time considered sending Agee to the Harvard Business School. "That story," Luce wrote to me in 1964, "is quite plausible—though I do not actually recall it. A problem in journalism that interested me then—and still does—is to combine good writing and 'human understanding' with familiarity with business." Eventually Luce gave up and the job went to someone else, but the article as it appeared in December retained traces of Jim's hand: "Caught across the green breadth of America like snail paths on a monstrous plantain leaf are 400,000 . . . steel miles. If, under the maleficent influence of that disorderly phosphorus which all steel contains, every inch of this bright mileage were suddenly to thaw into thin air. . . ."

6

During that fall and winter and the following year we pretty often had lunch or dinner together. I would call for him in his lofty office, or I would look up over my typewriter in the newspaper city room where by that time I worked and see him coming down the aisle from the elevator. He would come at his fast, loose, long-legged walk, springy on the balls of his feet, with his open overcoat flapping. We would go to a saloon for beer and roast beef sandwiches. I wish very badly that I could recall the conversations of those times, because in them we found our particular kind of brotherhood. Both of us had been deeply enchanted and instructed, and were both skilled, in an art remote from news writing, an art that we were not getting time or breath to practice much. You would underestimate us if you supposed that we met to exchange grievances, for of these in the ordinary sense we had none. We met to exchange perceptions, and I had then and later the sense that neither of us felt himself more fully engaged than in talk with the other. My own childhood enabled me to understand his, in particular his schooling at the monastery school of Saint Andrew's in Tennessee. We were both in the habit of looking into the shadow of Death. Although we came of different stock and from different regions, we were both Catholic (he, to be precise, Anglo-Catholic) by bringing-up and metaphysical formation; both dubious not to say distressed about "Church"; both inclined to the "religion of art," meaning that no other purpose, as we would have put it, seemed worth a damn in comparison with making good poems. Movies, of course, we talked about a good deal. My experience was not as wide as his, my passion less, but we admired certain things in common: Zasu Pitts in *Greed* and the beautiful sordidness of that film; the classic flight down the flights of steps in *Potemkin;* Keaton; Chaplin. We saw, sometimes together, and "hashed over," as Jim would say, the offerings of that period: the René Clairs, the Ernst Lubitsches; *The Informer; Man of Aran; Grand Illusion; Mayerling; The Blue Angel; Maedchen in Uniform; Zwei Herzen.*

The various attitudes covered by "taking care of yourself" interested Jim Agee, but rarely to the point of making him experiment with any. Rubbers, for example, he probably thought shameful and never wore in his adult life; on the contrary, in that period, his shoes both winter and summer were often worn through, with cracked uppers. But he had some conventional habits and impulses. He wore a hat, a small one that rode high on his shock of dark hair. For several entire weeks in 1934 he gave up cigarettes for a pipe. The episode of the pipe was the last effort of that kind that he would make until many years later when he cut down smoking after his first heart attack.

Another thing he did with Via was to keep a catboat at City Island and go out there to sail and swim on Sundays in summer. I think he had been on the swimming team at Exeter; at any rate he had an enviable backstroke. On one of these Sunday excursions when I went along I remember that we amused ourselves during the long black blowy subway ride by playing the metaphor game: by turns each describing an inanimate object in such a way as to portray without naming a public figure. Jim developed a secondhand silver flute into Leslie Howard, and a Grand Rapids easy chair into Carl Sandburg. Later that evening we had a memorable and I suppose comic conversation about whether or not the Artist should Keep in Shape. In the course of this I quoted Rémy de Gourmont to the effect that a writer writes with his whole body, bringing immediate and delighted assent from Jim, but not to the inference I myself would draw. His own body seemed so rugged and his stamina so great that I thought he could overlook his health and get away with it. The truth is that he was not as rugged as he looked. He had an inclination to hemophilia that had nearly cost him his life when he had his tonsils out in 1928, and at Exeter, too, he had first hurt his heart trying to run the mile. He never mentioned any of this.

Many-tiered and mysterious, the life of the great city submerged us now, me rather more, since I had no eyrie like his, but all day long spanieled back and forth in it and at night battered at my deadlines; and I think Jim envied me the unpretentious but hard craft I had got into. Whatever other interests we had, one became fairly constant and in time inveterate: the precise relation between any given real situation or event and the versions of it presented in print, that is, after a number of accidents, processes, and conventions had come into play. The quite complicated question of "how it really was" came before us all the time, along with our resources and abilities for making any part of that actuality known in the frames our employers gave us. Of those frames we were acutely aware, being acutely aware of others more adequate. Against believing most of what I read I am armored to this day with defenses worked out in those years and the years to follow. Styles, of course, endlessly interested us, and one of Jim's notions was that of writing an entire false issue of the *World Telegram* dead-pan, with every news item and ad heightened in its own style to the point of parody. He could easily have done it. Neither of us felt snide about eyewitness writing in itself or as practiced by Lardner or Hemingway; how could we? We simply mistrusted the journalistic apparatus as a mirror of the world, and we didn't like being consumed by it. Neither of us ever acquired a professional and equable willingness to work in that harness. For him to do so would have been more difficult than for me, since he had a great talent for prose fiction and I had not. After being turned down for the Guggenheim, in fact, he thought of trying to publish a book of his stories, and went so far as to write a preface for it.

"I shall do my best to stick to people in this book," he wrote. "That may seem to you the least I could do; but the fact is, I'm so tied up with symbols and half-abstractions and many issues about poetry which we'd better steer clear of now, that it is very hard for me to see people clearly as people. . . . Someday, if my life is worth anything, I shall hope to give people clearly in clear poetry, and to make them not real in the usual senses of real, but more than that: full of vitality and of the ardor of their own truth."

But he dropped the idea of publishing any stories at that point. Instead, with MacLeish's encouragement, he gathered the best of his old poems together with some new ones to make a book, and in October, 1934, in the Yale Younger Poets series, in which MacLeish and Stephen Vincent Benét were then interested, the Yale Press published *Permit Me Voyage*.

7

Of how I felt about Jim's book then, it is perhaps enough to say that at bad times in the next year or two I found some comfort in being named in it. So far as I can discover, none of the contemporary comments on it, including the foreword by MacLeish, took much notice of what principally distinguished it at the time: the religious terms and passion of several pieces, rising at times to the grand manner. In two of his three pages MacLeish did not refer to the book at all, being engaged in arguing that neither of the current literary "programs," America Rediscovered and Capitalism Be Damned, mattered in comparison with *work* done. As to Agee, "Obviously he has a deep love of the land. Equally obviously he has a considerable contempt for the dying civilization in which he has spent twenty-four years." But he said nothing of the fact that Agee's book appeared to be the work of a desperate Christian; in fact, he rather insisted on saying nothing, for he concluded that by virtue of the poet's gift, especially his ear, and his labor at his art, "the work achieves an integral and inward importance altogether independent of the opinions and purposes of its author."

This was true enough, but some of the poems were so unusual in what they suggested as to call, you might think, for a word of recognition. One gusty day years later, as we were crossing 49th Street, Jim and I halted in the Radio City wind and sunlight to agree with solemnity on a point of mutual and long-standing wonderment, not to say consternation: how rarely people seem to believe that a serious writer means it; he means what he says or what he discloses. Love for the land certainly entered into *Permit Me Voyage;* contempt for a dying civilization much less, and contempt here was not quite the word. It could even be said, on the contrary, that a sequence of twenty-five regular and in some cases truly metaphysical sonnets rather honored that civilization, insofar as a traditional verse form could represent it. The most impressive things in the book were the "Dedication" and the "Chorale," and what were these but strenuous prayers? They could have no importance, because no existence, independent of the opinions and purposes of the author.

A sense of the breathing community immersed in mystery, exposed to a range of experience from what can only be called the divine to what can only be called the diabolical, most intelligent in awe and most needful of mercy—a religious sense of life, in short—moved James Agee in his best work. If in introducing that work the sensitive and well-disposed MacLeish could treat this motive as unmentionable, that may give some idea of where Agee stood amid the interests and pressures of the time. It must be added that those interests were also Agee's, and that those pressures he not only profoundly felt but himself could bring to bear.

Four years at Harvard had complicated out of recognition his youthful Episcopalianism (he preferred to say Catholicism), but he hated polite academic agnosticism to the bone. In one *Advocate* editorial as a senior he had even proposed Catholicism as desirable for undergraduates. The poem, *John Carter,* that he had begun there, and would have carried on if he could, was to be an "anatomy of evil" wrought, he said, by an agent of evil in the "orthodox Roman Catholic" sense. At twenty-five, after two years in New York, he published an openly religious book of poems. MacLeish was not alone in ignoring what it said; the reviewers also ignored it. It was as if the interests and pressures of the time made it inaudible.

Inaudible? Since I still find it difficult to read the "Dedication" and the "Chorale" without feeling a lump in my throat, I do not understand this even now. If he had been heard, surely a twinge of compunction would have crossed the hearts of thousands. But the book itself, Jim's poems in general, remained very little known or remarked during his lifetime, and for that matter are little known even now. One reason for this, I am well aware, is that in the present century the rhymed lyric and the sonnet for a time seemed disqualified as "modern poetry." Jim was aware of it, too; so aware that his sequence ended with a farewell to his masters, the English poets: "My sovereign souls, God grant my sometime brothers, I must desert your ways now if I can." The concluding poem in the book, the title poem, was indeed a conclusion, but it enfolded a purpose. "My heart and mind discharted lie—" with reference, that is, to the compass points, religious, literary, and other, within which at Saint Andrew's, at Exeter, at Harvard and in New York he had by and large lived and worked. This was more than the usual boredom of the artist with work that is over and done with. He turned away now from Christian thought and observance, and began to turn away from the art of verse. Yet his purpose was to rechart, to reorient himself, by reference to the compass needle itself, his own independent power of perception, his own soul.

8

Therein such strong increase to find
In truth as is my fate to know.

Everyone who knew Jim Agee will remember that in these years there grew upon him what became habitual almost to idiosyncrasy: a way of tilting any subject every which way in talk, with prolonged and exquisite elaboration and scruple. He was after the truth, the truth about specific events or things, and the truth about his own impressions and feelings. By truth I mean what he would chiefly mean: correspondence between what is said and what is the case—but what is the case at the utmost reach of consciousness. Now this intent has been delicately and justly distinguished from the intent of art, which is to make, not to state, things; and a self-dedication to truth on the part of Shakespeare or Mozart (Ageean examples) would indeed strike us as peculiar. On the other hand, with philosophy dethroned and the rise of great Realists, truth-telling has often seemed to devolve almost by default upon the responsible writer, enabling everyone else to have it both ways: his truth as truth if they want it, or as something else if they prefer, since after all he is merely an artist. Jim Agee, by nature an artist and responsive to all the arts, took up this challenge to perceive in full and to present immaculately what was the case.

Think of all that conspired to make him do so. The place of Truth in that awareness of the living God that he had known as a child and young man and could not forget. The place of truth at the university, *Veritas,* perennial object of the scholar's pains. New techniques for finding out what was the case: among them, in particular, sociological study, works like *Middletown* in the United States and *Mass Observation* in England, answering to the perplexity of that age, and the "documentary" by which the craft of the cameraman could show forth unsuspected lineaments of the actual. (An early and what would appear a commonplace example of this craft, *The River,* by Pare Lorentz, excited Agee and myself.) Then, to sicken and enrage him, there was the immense new mud-fall of falsehood over the world, not ordinary human lying and dissimulation but a calculated barrage, laid down by professional advertisers and propagandists, to corrupt people by the continent-load. Finally, day by day, he had the given occupation of journalism, ostensibly and usually in good faith concerned with what was the case. In the editing of *Fortune* all the other factors played a part: the somewhat missionary zeal of the Founder, a certain respect for standards of scholarship, a sociological interest in looking into the economic conditions and mode of life of classes and crafts in America, an acquiescence in advertising and in self-advertisement, and, of course, photography.

The difficulties of the period were, however, deepened by an intellectual dismay, not entirely well-founded but insidious under many forms: *What was the case* in some degree proceeded from the observer. Theoretical in abstract thought for centuries, this cat seemed now to have come out of the bag to bewitch all knowledge in practice: knowledge of microcosmic entities, of personal experience, of human society. Literary art had had to reckon with it. To take an elementary example, Richards would put three x's on a blackboard disposed thus .˙. to represent poem, referent, and reader, suggesting that a complete account of the poem could no more exclude one x than another, nor the relationship between them. Nor were the x's stable, but variable. *Veritas* had become tragically complicated. The naïve practices of journalism might continue, as they had to, but their motives and achievements, like all others, appeared now suspect to Freudian and Marxian and semanticist alike; and of what these men believed they understood, James Agee was (or proposed to make himself) also aware. Hence his self-examinations, his ambivalences ("split" feelings) on so many things. As he realized well enough, they could become tedious, but they were crucial to him and had the effect that what he knew, in the end, he knew with practiced definition. It must be added that the more irritated and all-embracing and scrupulous his aspiration to full truth, "objective" and "subjective" at once, the more sharply he would know his own sinful vainglory or Pride in that ambition, in those scruples; and he did. Few men were more sensitive to public and private events than he was, and he would now explore and discriminate among them with his great appetite, his energy, his sometimes paralyzing conscience, and the intellect that Richards had alerted. I am of course reducing a long and tentative and often interrupted effort into a few words.

I named three books arbitrarily as stars principal in our first years at Harvard; I will name three more, arbitrarily again, to recall the planetary influences after graduation. In the spring of 1934, after Judge Wolsey's decision, Random House published *Ulysses* for the first time legally in America, and even if we had read it before, as Jim and I had, in the big Shakespeare & Co. edition, we could and did now read it again, in a handier form suitable for carrying on the subway. Or for the Agee bathroom, where I remember it. Joyce engrossed him and got into his blood so thoroughly that in 1935 he felt obliged, as he told a friend of mine, to master and get over that influence if he were ever to do anything of his own.

Céline's *Voyage au Bout de la Nuit* was our first taste of the end-of-the-rope writing that became familiar later in Miller and later still in Beckett. Malraux's *Man's Fate* had another special position. This story, with Auden's early poems, counted as much as the Russian movies of Eisenstein and Dovzhenko in swaying Jim toward communism. The attraction in any case was strong. The peaceful Roosevelt revolution had only begun; there was a real clash of classes in America. I had myself, in a single day of reporting, seen the pomp of high capitalism to be faded and phoney at an NAM convention in the Waldorf, and the energies of laboring men to be robust and open at a union meeting. On one side of his nature Jim was a frontiersman and a Populist to whom blind wealth and pretentious gentility were offensive. Besides this he had the Romantic artist's contempt, "considerable contempt," for the Philistine and for what were then known to us as bourgeois attitudes—though he distinguished between the human souls that inherited them. For poverty and misery in general he had a sharp-eyed pity. The idea of a dedicated brotherhood working underground in the ghastly world held his imagination for several years—spies amid the enemy, as Auden had imagined them; at the same time he had no great difficulty in seeing through most of the actual candidates for such a brotherhood, including himself. The Party fished in vain for Agee, who by liking only what was noble in the revolution liked too little of it.

9

Embedded in *Fortune* for those years are several of Jim's best efforts at telling how things really were. As in the description of the Tennessee River, these are most often concerned with American landscapes and American living. In September, 1934, for example, there was this opening to an article on the Great American Roadside:

> This continent, an open palm frank before the sky against the bulk of the world. This curious people. The automobile you know as well as you know the slouch of the accustomed body at the wheel and the small stench of gas and hot metal. You know the sweat and the steady throes of the motor and the copious and thoughtless silence and the almost lack of hunger and the spreaded swell and swim of the hard highway toward and beneath and behind and gone and the parted roadside swarming past. This great road, too; you know that well. How it is scraggled and twisted along the coast of Maine, high-crowned and weak-shouldered in honor of long winter. How in Florida the detours are bright with the sea-lime of rolled shells. How the stiff wide stream of hard unbroken roadstead spends the mileage between Mexicali and Vancouver. How the road degrades into a rigorous lattice of country dirt athwart Kansas through the smell of hot wheat and this summer a blindness and a strangulation of lifted dust. How like a blacksnake in the sun it takes the ridges, the green and dim ravines which are the Cumberlands, and lolls loose into the hot Alabama valleys. How in the spectral heat of the Southwest, and the wide sweeps of saga toward the Northwest, it means

spare fuel strapped to the runing board. . . . Oh yes, you know this road; and you know this roadside. You know this roadside as well as you know the formulas of talk at the gas station, the welcome taste of a Bar-B-Q sandwich in midafternoon, the oddly excellent feel of a weak-springed bed in a clapboard transient shack, and the early start in the cold bright lonesome air, the dustless and dewy road.

In October of the same year, on the Drought:

> That this has been by all odds the most ruinous drought in U.S. history is old stuff to you by now. So are the details, as the press reported them, week by broiling week, through the summer. But all the same, the chances are strong that you have no idea what the whole thing meant: what, simply and gruesomely, it was. Really to know, you should have stood with a Dakota farmer and watched a promissory rack of cloud take the height of the sky, weltering in its lightnings . . . and the piteous meager sweat on the air, and the earth baked stiff and steaming. You should have been a lot more people in a lot more places, really to know. Barring that impossibility, however, there is the clear dispassionate eye of the camera, which under honest guidance has beheld these bitter and these transient matters, and has recorded this brutal season for the memory of easier time to come.

These quotations must suffice, and they are not carelessly chosen. In 1935 he did a thorough re-examination of the TVA, published in May, and a study of Saratoga, New York, published in August. These and other examples of sheer ability won him a taste of the freedom he craved. Beginning in November, *Fortune* gave him a six months' leave of absence, most of which he and Via spent in Florida on a small coastal island, Anna Maria, south of St. Petersburg and Tampa.

In a notebook of his, half-filled with jottings of that winter, I find the first entry amusing at this distance: it was a name and an address—*The New Masses*—later canceled out by a scribble. He was now steadily devouring Freud and recording his dreams. "Read Freud until midnight" is an entry several times repeated. There are pages like Stephen's or

Bloom's waking thoughts in *Ulysses.* There are notes and self-injunctions about writing. For instance:

> My need for tone, tension & effect in writing limits me very badly. Yet cd. be good. But in many ways needless effort. And in many ways false. Its attempt in long run: to give, at once, frame and fluescence to pic. of universe. Seem to feel I have no right to give the looseness till is established the tightness wherein it moves. . . . Must throw brain into detail. And into fearlessness, shamelessness & naturalness abt writing. . . . Poem or prose in line between The Barge She Sat In and a social report of a wedding. What was worn. Who was there. etc. / Bks not of one thing—stories, poetry, essays, etc. / but of all, down to most casual.

In December he wrote some ottava rima, a few stanzas mocking something Sir Samuel Hoare, then British foreign minister, had said in the course of diplomacy that winter over the Italian war against Ethiopia. It was the last spasm of *John Carter.* He read *Crime and Punishment,* Caroline Spurgeon on *Shakespeare's Imagery,* and *The Counterfeiters.* Gide, he wrote,

> . . . makes me realize more clearly than I have for a long time what a damned soft and uncertain customer I am. Had again, still have, though now my head and purposes are woolly, feeling of necessity to go plain to the bone and stay there. The 40-day fasts and that kind of thing. Misnamed virtues: they clear you: which is a state of grace or virtue. / Virtual / feel in many words, suddenly like little puffs of light, nowadays, the shine and silver quality wh. is equivalent (EQUIVALENT is such a word) to a whole certain tone in Bach. Does Bach and don't many composers reduce to 2 or 3 dominant tones? & I don't mean idioms either. Same with writers. Mozart's very skillful chromatic developments & returns that an ear holds a lot less surely than much trickier 20th Century stuff. Analyze (can you) quality of excitement in minuet of Jupiter. Sense of a full orchestra in a Beethovenish way of being full, even in 1st measure when woodwinds have it. Mozart's queer "darker" music, something like Hopkins' love of the dappled, the counter, original, spare, strange. In some rather

homely themes of scherzi—and, likelier to turn up in them than in slo mvts & finales? 1st mvt of G-minor has some of it, too. Also vide great values of the prosy & verbose line in poetry, & of bromide almost. Note some of Mozart's more strenuous & some of his more tossed off slow mvts; lyrics in Songs of Innocence; many passages in Schubert; quite a few in Beethoven.

Among many entries on music, there is one noting "the great beauty of West End Blues" and another, written firmly with a fresh pencil as if he wanted badly to get it down:

> Swing music is different from any contemporary Art Mouthpiece. Barring straight folk stuff and vaude & burlesk adlibbing, runs roughly this way. Writing last had this freedom in Elizabeth's time, with something half like it but crippled in Byron. Sculpture of Africans has it. Music lost it (roughly) with Mozart. Beethoven had but did not use and finally buried it. The 19th and 20th centuries are solidly self-conscious and inhibited. Only swing today is perfectly free and has in its kind a complete scope. Some directors have it. Eisenstein does or did. Disney does or did. Chaplin did. There may be bits of it in some surrealist art. With words, does Perelman have some? and Groucho some? and Durante some? But all pretty much of a kind: not at all capable of wonderful lyric scope of swing. Can words spoken or written possibly break through it again, break through and get free.

He worked on some of the poems that were published over the next three years or so, on some that were never published or worth publishing, on others that have not survived. He drafted autobiographical material that would serve him years later in the novel published after his death, as the following entry indicated: "Have been working (c. 12–15,000 words) on the footloose in Knoxville idea. Don't know." One entry of great importance, because it stated an obsession that had its relevance to everything and especially to "Church" and Christianity, was this: "Truth goes much less far than falsehood: at every transition, more misunderstanding comes aboard: gradually becomes handleable by those too corrupted by falsehood to handle bare truth. Radium into lead."] I have been quoting these notes generously in the hope that you will hear at least remotely a voice in them and get at least an inkling of what his talk was like. But one final entry I will quote as a thing in itself, comparable to one of Hopkins' beautifully delineated studies of nature in the *Notebooks*. This was during a walk on a misty night under an almost full moon down the beach on Anna Maria.

> Surf as rounded point, coming in at acute angle, running along its edges on shallow sand with tearing glistening sound, like drawn zipper opening. Then around pt., meet surf broadside. In darkness you see it, well out on the dark, explode like opening parachute, and come in. Another kind: where in 2–3 parts on single line it whitens and the white widens—again the glistening zipper action—till all white meets and in it comes. Also: smallish tendons of it, private to themselves, bearing up (no white) and smacking themselves straight down on hard sand beneath a few inches of water with great passion and impact, PFFUHHH. Also, lovely and violent, competent folding-under of seam, pursing as of lips, when wave crest falls so prematurely as to undermine its own back: so you get a competent, systematic turning under in long lines. Also sink and drying of water in sand as shallow wave draws down.

10

In May, 1936, some time before the great day of the assignment in Alabama, Jim and I journeyed together to Bennington to read our verses to the college. In that budding grove he was almost inaudible, as usual when reading his own or other poems, but then as a kind of encore he did a parody of a southern preacher in a hellfire sermon, and this was more than audible: it brought down the house. I have not found it in manuscript, but I have included in this book a prose parody of the same period, to show the sort of thing he occasionally did. You do not hear much of his parodies. You do not hear much, either, of his mimetic powers, great as they were, though years later he had a bit part as a "vagrant" in one of his movies. At the time I am thinking of, one of his best acts was a recital of "When the lamp is shattered" in the accent and pitch of rural Tennessee.

We saw a good deal of one another all that spring—by this time I was married and working for *Time*—but by midsummer he was gone into the Deep South with Walker Evans on the tenant farmer job. Walker has written very well about that in his short foreword to the 1960 reissue of *Let Us Now Praise Famous Men.*

Jim's passionate eye for the lighted world made him from boyhood a connoisseur of photography, and among all photographers I think the one who had moved him most was Mathew Brady. The portraits and Civil War photographs of Brady were a kind of absolute for him, calling him and sounding in him very deeply. Another near-absolute was the photography in von Stroheim's *Greed;* he especially loved the burning-white powdery kind of sunlight produced by the "orthochromatic" film of that period. These kinds of studied finality and fiery delicacy in images of contemporary existence he found above all in the photographs of Walker Evans. Their work together that summer made them collaborators and close friends for life. It is strange that Jim never wrote much about Evans' photographs. Perhaps this was because only a couple of years later the Museum of Modern Art held a big Evans exhibition for which Lincoln Kirstein wrote a full and handsome introduction. Jim did write, in 1942, an introduction for a proposed book of photographs by another artist he admired, Helen Levitt. For a full and pondered statement of what photography meant to him, you will do well to consult this book, *A Way of Seeing,* finally published in 1965 by the Viking Press. The heart of what he wrote is this:

> The artist's task [in photography] is not to alter the world as the eye sees it into a world of esthetic reality, but to perceive the esthetic reality within the actual

world, and to make an undisturbed and faithful record of the instant in which this movement of creativeness achieves its most expressive crystallization. Through his eye and through his instrument the artist has, thus, a leverage upon the materials of existence which is unique.

After the summer in Alabama I should guess that he got his *Fortune* piece done in September or October, and I remember it hanging fire in the autumn, but I can't be sure of these dates. Why did the magazine in the end reject the article that the editor, knowing Agee and therefore presumably knowing more or less what to expect, had assigned him to write? Well, one reason was very simple: the editor was no longer the same man. He was no longer the same man because *Fortune*'s repute in the Duquesne Club and the Sky Club and the Bohemian Club—in those places, in short, where subscribers met—had been damaged by what appeared to the subscribers as a leftward drift in the contents of the magazine. In 1935 Jim's piece might have been printed, but in 1936, by the excellent disposition of Providence, the new editor, not much liking his duty, did his duty and turned it down.

Now all hands at last had more than a glimmer of a fact I have alluded to earlier—that Agee's vocation, at least at that point and as up to that point meditated by himself and inflamed by his recent experience, was in competition with *Fortune*. It appeared that the magazine, committed of course to knowing what was the case, had had the offhand humanity and imagination and impertinence to send an ex-president of the Harvard *Advocate* into the helpless and hopeless lives of cotton tenant farmers, but that it did not have the courage to face in full the case he presented, since the case involved discomfort not only for the tenants but for *Fortune*. Anything but that. Well and good, this gave him his chance to show *Fortune* and everyone else how to treat the case: he would make the assignment his own and make a book of his own on the tenant farmers. His friend Edward Aswell at Harper

& Bros. induced that firm to offer Agee and Evans a contract and an advance, but for the time being Jim did not accept it, fearing that it might affect the writing. He remained loosely attached to *Fortune.* I believe no high words passed.

In 1937 he was in and out of the office on three jobs. The most interesting took him to Havana on an excruciating Caribbean "vacation cruise," of which his narrative, appearing in September as "Six Days at Sea," was a masterpiece of ferocity, or would have been if it had been printed uncut. He had become grimmer about American middle-class ways and destinies, and would become grimmer still. His inclination to simple cleanliness, for example, turned to anger for awhile as he discerned meanness and status and sterility even in that.

In the good poems of this period, the one to his father in *Transition,* the one called "Sunday: Outskirts of Knoxville," and some of the lyrics in the *Partisan Review,* he did things unachieved in *Permit Me Voyage.* But most of the topical poems in quatrains, published or unpublished, are not so good. He never did as well in this vein as in the epigrammatic "Songs on the Economy of Abundance" that he had sent to Louis Untermeyer for the 1936 edition of *Modern American Poetry.* His skill with traditional meters declined; it remained, now, mistrusted and for long periods unused, or used only casually and briefly. The Auden-MacNeice *Letters from Iceland* came out that year with a section of brilliant Byronics, and if Jim had had any intention of going on with *John Carter*—as I believe that by now he did not—those pages might have dissuaded him. Auden's unapproachable virtuosity may, in fact, have had something—not much, but inevitably something—to do with Jim's writing verse more seldom. "Seen this?" he came in saying one day, with a new book in his hand, and read aloud the Auden poem that opens with such beauty:

Out on the lawn I lie in bed,
Vega conspicuous overhead,
In the windless nights of June . . .

In the Bickford's Cafeteria at Lexington and 43rd, over coffee at some small hour of the morning, we read together and recognized perfection in a set of new lyrics by Robert Frost in the *Atlantic;* one was the short one beginning: "I stole forth dimly in the dripping pause/Between two downpours to see what there was." Perfection of this order Jim now scarcely any longer tried for in verse.

Under one strain and another his marriage was now breaking up; I remember the summer day in 1937 when at his suggestion we met in Central Park for lunch and the new young woman in her summer dress appeared. It seems to me that there were months of indecisions and revisions and colloquies over the parting with Via, which was yet not to be a parting, etc., which at length would be accomplished as cruelly required by the laws of New York. Laceration could not have been more prolonged. In the torments of liberty all Jim's friends took part. At Old Field Point on the north shore of Long Island, where the Wilder Hobsons had somehow rented a bishop's boathouse that summer, a number of us attained liberation from the *pudor* of mixed bathing without bathing suits: a mixed pleasure, to tell the truth.

One occasion in this period that I remember well was a public meeting held in June, 1937, in Carnegie Hall, by a "Congress of American Writers," a Popular Front organization, for the Spanish Loyalist cause. Jim and I went to this together, and as we took our seats he turned to me and said, "Know one writer you can be sure isn't here? Cummings." MacLeish spoke, very grave. His speech was a prophetic one in which he might very well have quoted "Ask not for whom the bell tolls: it tolls for thee." Then he introduced Hemingway. It must have been the only time in his life that Hemingway consented to couple with a lectern, and as a matter of fact he only stood beside it and leaned on it with one elbow. Bearish in a dark blue suit, one foot cocked over the other, he gave a running commentary to a movie documentary by Joris Ivens on a Spanish town under the Republic. Jim Agee hoped for the Republic, but I don't think he ever saluted anyone with a raised fist or took up Spanish (my own gesture—belated at that). He had joined battle on another ground.

In October he put in his second vain application for a Guggenheim Fellowship. His "Plans for Work" (of which he kept a carbon) are printed in this book and will give you an idea of his mood at the time, maverick and omnivorous as a prairie fire, ranging in every direction for What Was the Case and techniques for telling it. As in 1932 he did not fail to indulge in those gratuitous honesties (now about communism, for instance) that would make it tough for the Guggenheim committee. I do not know how he lived that winter, or lived through it.

Not, however, till the spring of 1938 did he take the Harper's contract and settle down with Alma Mailman, in a small frame house at 27 Second Street, Frenchtown, New Jersey, to write or rewrite and construct his book. Jim wrote for the ear, wanted criticism from auditors, and read to me, either in Frenchtown or in New York, most of the drafts as he got them written. There isn't a word in *Let Us Now Praise Famous Men* that he—and I and others—did not ponder many times. Frenchtown was then quiet and deep in the dense countryside, traversable whenever and as far as necessary in an ancient open flivver; they had a goat, God knows how acquired, in the backyard; there was a tennis court in the town. Jim played an obstinate and mighty game, but wild, against my obstinate and smoother one.

He labored all summer and fall, through the Sudeten crisis and the international conferences and the Nazi mass meetings at Nuremberg and elsewhere that sent the strangled shouting of *Der Führer* and *Sieg Heil, Sieg Heil* in an ominous rhythmic roar over the radios of the country. He labored into the winter. I have found among his things a journal in which he noted on December 1st that when the rent was paid

he would have $12.52 in the world and in the same breath went on with plans for his wedding to Alma later that month. In January or February *Fortune* came to the rescue with an assignment: the section on Brooklyn in an issue to be devoted to New York City. For the rest of the winter and spring they moved to a flat in St. James Place, taking the goat with them.

When Wilder Hobson went to see them once he found that the neighborhood kids had chalked on the front steps: "The Man Who Lives Here is a Loony."

11

In the living room or backyard of that place I heard several drafts of his prose on Brooklyn, and by some

accident kept two drafts in a file. Twenty-four years later these turned out to be the only vestiges of this work in existence. In this case, too, *Fortune* found Jim's article too strong to print and it did not appear in the New York issue (June, 1939). *Fortune's* editor, however, appreciated this labor. As epigraph to

the tamer article (by someone else) that finally got into print, the editor lifted one lyric sentence from Jim's piece and quoted it, with attribution. The version printed in this book is Jim's preliminary draft: *Southeast of the Island: Travel Notes.* The later version prepared for *Fortune* editing on May 15, 1939 (by the "ditto" process, which produced a number of legible copies) was shorter by nearly half and lacked the particularity of the earlier piece. Compression and generality served him well in one passage only, funny and biting if you remember that *Fortune* was rather given to Ripley-like statistical play:

> Courtship and marriage are difficult matters to speak of, and it will be the better part of valor not to speak of them, beyond remarking that no park has ever been more eloquently designed beneath the moon for its civic purpose than Prospect; that more homes are owned in Brooklyn than elsewhere in New York City; that there are more children per capita; that the divorce rate is only . . . per cent per head that of Manhattan; that there are 48,000 electric refrigerators in Flatbush alone; and that if all the perambulators in Brooklyn were pushed end to end, at the pace of a walking mother, they would soon reach three times around the origin of species, the history of religion, the cause of imperialistic war, sexual ethics and social fear, and the basis of private property and universal prenatal spiritual suffocation.

After the Brooklyn interlude, the Agees returned to Frenchtown for the summer. Some weeks before we heard Mr. Chamberlain's weary voice declaring that a state of war existed between His Majesty's Government and Nazi Germany, Jim Agee's manuscript of a book entitled *Three Tenant Families* was in the hands of the publishers. The war began, and the German armored divisions shot up Poland. In the Harper offices Jim's manuscript must have appeared a doubtful prospect as a rousing topical publishing event. The publishers wanted him to make a few domesticating changes. He would not make the changes. Harper's then deferred publication; they could live without it. He was broke and in debt, and in the early fall he learned that fatherhood impended for him in the spring. I had just fallen heir to the job of "Books" editor at *Time,* so we arranged that he should join me and the other reviewer, Calvin Fixx, at writing the weekly book section, and he and Alma found a flat far over on the west side somewhere below 14th Street.

Now for eight or nine months we worked in the same office several days and/or nights a week. Early that year or maybe late the year before, I can't remember precisely when, the Luce magazines had moved to a new building called the Time & Life Building in Rockefeller Center between 48th and 49th Streets (now superseded by a later and of course bigger and better T & L Building farther west). We had a three-desk office on the twenty-eighth floor with a secretary's cubbyhole. Our secretary, or "checker," was a girl I had known in 1934 when she was Lewis Gannett's secretary on the *Herald Tribune*—a crap-shooting hoydenish girl who used to get weekly twenty-page letters from a lonely and whimsical young man in a San Francisco YMCA, by the name, then unknown, of William Saroyan. In the years between 1934 and 1939 Mary had been in South Africa and had come back statelier but still *au fond* not giving a damn; her father was an Episcopal canon. She kept track of the review books and publication dates and spotted errors in what we wrote. The other reviewer, Fixx, was a Mormon, a decent, luminously inarticulate man engaged in living down some obscure involvement in the Far Left. He knew a great deal about that particular politics and history, now a great subject for "re-evaluation" after the Ribbentrop-Molotov embrace. Each of us read half-a-dozen books a week and wrote reviews or notes—or nothing—according to our estimates of each.

Jim Agee of course added immeasurably to the pleasure of this way of life. If for any reason a book interested him (intentionally or unintentionally on the author's part) he might write for many hours about it, turning in many thousands of words. Some of these long and fascinating reviews would rebound from the managing editor in the form of a paragraph. We managed nevertheless to hack through that barrier a fairly wide vista on literature in general, including even verse, the despised quarterlies, and scholarship. With light hearts and advice of counsel we reviewed a new edition of the classic *Wigmore on Evidence*. One week we jammed through a joint review of Henry Miller, for which Jim did *Tropic of Cancer* and I *Tropic of Capricorn*, both unpublishable in the United States until twenty years later. Our argument that time was that if *Time* ought to be written for the Man-in-the-Street (a favorite thought of the Founder), here were books that would hit him where he lived, if he could get them. In all our efforts we were helped by T. S. Matthews, then a senior editor and later for six years managing editor and a friend to Jim Agee.

Not because I idolize Jim or admire every word he ever wrote but again to show his mind at work, this time in that place under those conditions, I will quote the first paragraph of his review of Herbert Gorman's *James Joyce* and the final paragraphs from his review of *The Hamlet* by William Faulkner.

> The utmost type of heroism, which alone is worthy of the name, must be described, merely, as complete self-faithfulness: as integrity. On this level the life of James Joyce has its place, along with Blake's and Beethoven's among the supreme examples. It is almost a Bible of what a great artist, an ultimately honest man, is up against.

> Whatever their disparities, William Faulkner and William Shakespeare share these characteristics: 1) Their abundance of invention and their courage for rhetoric are bottomless. 2) Enough goes on in their heads to furnish a whole shoal of more temperate writers. 3) By fair means or foul, both manage to play not for a specialized but for a broad audience.
>
> In passages incandescent with undeniable genius,

there is [in *The Hamlet*] nevertheless not one sentence without its share of amateurishness, its stain of inexcusable cheapness.

12

Of the physical make and being of James Agee and his aspect at that time, you must imagine: a tall frame, long-boned but not massive; lean flesh, muscular with some awkwardness; pelt on his chest; a long stride with loose knee-joints, head up, with toes angled a bit outward. A complexion rather dark or sallow in pigment, easily tanned. The head rough-hewn, with a rugged brow and cheek-bones, a strong nose irregular in profile, a large mouth firmly closing in folds, working a little around the gaps of lost teeth. The shape of the face tapered to a sensitive chin, cleft. Hair thick and very dark, a shock uncared for, and best uncared for. Eyes deep-set and rather closely set, a dull gray-blue or feral blue-gray or radiantly lit with amusement. Strong stained teeth. On the right middle finger a callous as big as a boil: one of his stigmata as a writer. The hands and fingers long and light and blunt and expressive, shaping his thought in the air, conveying stresses direct or splay, drawing razor-edged lines with thumb and forefinger: termini, perspective, tones.

His capacity for whiskey, as for everything else, was very great. I saw him once or twice violent with drink, but I never saw him disabled by it and don't know anyone else who ever did. As a rule, with every drink he only became more interested in any subject or line of action—any except going home and going to bed. A little conviviality was enough to get his comic genius off the ground and into such flights as his one-man rendition of the Bach Toccata and Fugue as arranged by Stokowski—a magistral act in which varieties of fruity instrumentation were somehow conveyed by voice and gesture, e.g., the string section by a flapping left hand and "fiddle-faddle, fiddle-faddle, fiddle-faddle." At the invention of American place names, or personal names, Jim had no peer; one of his best compositions, brought off while wandering late at night with Wilder Hobson, was the man's name, "George F. Macgentsroom." Very rarely, he might follow through with an inspiration from one of those evenings. In his war against middle-class folkways he struck a happily premeditated blow at the Christmas card custom by sending out, one Christmas, a card bearing as its olde winter scene a photograph of a pair of polar bears in innocent copulation, with season's greetings.

At the piano he sat well back and more than erect, head withdrawn and watchful, eyes downcast over the length of arms and fingers in hard exertion at the keyboard. It was the old upright that his grandmother had given him; I think he had it for twenty years. When he played he would have the whole form of the sonata or whatever it was before him in his mind. Battered conclamant notes, quite a few near misses, very little sweet shading or pianissimo. At his writing he looked the same: his left hand pinning down at arm's length a stack of yellow second sheets, leaning far back from it frowning (by this time he was getting far-sighted; he tried, but discarded, some steel-rimmed glasses), power flowing through the sharp pencil into the tiny closely organized script. Wholly focused on it, as I remember him in warm weather once, oblivious to the closed office window behind him, stifling in a fog of cigarette smoke, with a small pure space cleared before him amid mountains of litter.

He wore blue or khaki work shirts and under the armpits there would be stains, salt-edged, from sweat; likewise under the arms of his suit jacket, double-breasted dark blue, wrinkled and shiny. He was too poor to afford a lot of laundering, and he didn't believe in it, anyway. After the baby arrived in March, 1940, I remember one big scene in which Jim was engaged in spooning Pablum into Joel. The father sat,

all elbows and knees, in an arm chair upholstered in some ragged and ancient fabric that had grown black absorbing through the years the grime of New York. The infant in his lap mouthed with a will at the Pablum but inevitably gobs of it splattered down even on the richly unsanitary arms of the chair, whence Jim would scoop it in long dives lest it drip—irretrievably, you could hope—on the floor.

The time was about over for all fragile arrangements and lightness of heart. In those days the German airborne troops were taking Norway. There was nothing we could do about it. One fine day in late spring, playing tennis with Jim on some courts south of Washington Square, I broke a bone in my instep. *Life* with a wealth of illustration assured us that General Gamelin was the flower of military science and the French army the finest in Europe. Within a week or so it looked as though *Life* had exaggerated. While I was still getting around on a plaster clubfoot the British were evacuating Dunkirk and the panzers were going through the Ardennes. The dress parade of the German army down the Champs-Elysées was reported by the *World-Telegram* with a photograph of the Arc de Triomphe and the headline ICI REPOSE UN SOLDAT FRANCAIS MORT POUR LA PATRIE. I looked at this and realized that so far as I was concerned a decade had come to an end, and so had a mode of life, to flatter it by that term, that included working for *Time.* To see what could be done about my *modus vivendi* in general, I turned over "Books" to Agee, Fixx, and Whittaker Chambers and departed, taking my first wife away to the west and eventually to Santa Fe for the winter. There I settled down on my savings to do unnecessary and unpaid work for the first time in five years. I had resigned. Taking no offense, and with great accuracy of foresight, the people at *Time* made it a leave of absence until a year from that October. I intrude these details because I am about to quote a few passages from Jim's letters to me during the year. At some point in the spring or summer Houghton Mifflin, to their eternal credit, accepted the manuscript that Harper's had released to him. Well, from a letter in December:

> Excepting Wilder, whose getting-a-job has done him a favor as leaving-it has you, everyone I see, myself included, is at a low grinding ebb of quiet desperation: nothing, in most cases, out of the ordinary, just the general average Thoreau was telling about, plus the dead-ends of one of the most evil years in history, plus each individual's little specialty act. I don't think I'll go into much if any detail—for though I could detail it blandly and painlessly and some of it is of "clinical" interest, it could possibly have an intrusive

and entangling effect. So I can most easily and honestly say that it isn't as bad as I've perhaps suggested, except by contrast with health and free action—is, in fact, just the average experience of people living as people shouldn't, where people shouldn't, doing what people shouldn't and little or nothing of what people should. Journalists, hacks, husbands, wives, sisters, neurotics, self-harmed artists, and such. Average New York Fall.

The book is supposed to be published January or February—no proofs yet, though. I now thoroughly regret using the subtitle (Let Us Now Praise Famous Men) as I should never have forgotten I would. I am rather anxious to look at it, finished and in print—possibly, also, to read it in that form—but I have an idea I'll be unable to stand to. If so, it might be a healthy self-scorching to force myself to: but that's probably my New England chapel-crank blood. Mainly, though, I want to be through with it, as I used to feel about absolution, and to get to work again as soon as I can. I am thirty-one now, and I can conceivably forgive myself my last ten years only by a devotion to work in the next ten which I suspect I'll be incapable of. I am much too vulnerable to human relationships, particularly sexual or in any case heterosexual, and much too deeply wrought-upon by them, and in turn much too dependent in my work on 'feeling' as against 'intellect.' In short I'm easily upset and, when upset, incapable of decent work; incapable of it also when I'm not upset enough. I must learn my ways in an exceedingly quiet marriage (which can be wonderful I've found but is basically not at all my style or apparent 'nature') or break from marriage and all close liaisons altogether and learn how to live alone & keep love at a bearable distance. Those are oddly juvenile things to be beginning to learn at my age: what really baffles me is that, knowing them quite well since I was 15, I've done such thorough jobs in the opposite direction. Well, nothing would be solved or even begun tonight by any thing I wrote or thought, or at any time soon: my business now and evidently for quite a while to come is merely to sit as tight and careful as I can, taking care above all to do no further harm to others or myself or my now virtually destroyed needs or hopes, and doing a timorous or drastic piece of mending when or wherever there seems any moment's chance to. I haven't been very intelligent—to say nothing of 'good'—and now it's scarcely a chance for intelligence or goodness—only for the most dumb and scrupulous tenacity. On the whole, though, it's time I had a good hard dose of bad going, and if I find I'm capable of it the winter will be less wasted than it otherwise might be. Meanwhile, though, I find I'm so dull I bore myself sick. A broken spirit and a contrite heart have their drawbacks: worst of all if at the same time the spirit is unbroken and ferocious and the heart contrite only in the sense of deep grief over pain and loss, not at all in true contrition. . . .

I thought *The Long Voyage Home* quite awful. . . .

I feel very glad you like the reviews. I wish I did. As a matter of fact I have hardly judgment or feeling, for or against, and on the whole, not a bad time with the job, except a general, rather shamed feeling, week by week, that with real intelligence & effort I could do much better, whatever the limitations of space and place. Then a book as important as Kafka's *America* can't even get reviewed, and I shrug it off again. . . .

The magazine you write of [an imaginary one—*R. F.*] makes my mouth water. I spend a lot of time thinking of such things and of equivalent publishers. They really existed in France and Germany and even in England. The fact that they don't here and I suppose won't ever, by any chance, makes me know just a little better what a fat-assed, frumpish hell-on-earth this country is. Last stronghold of just what. . . . But I do love to think about magazines like that. And the writing *can* be done—the only really important thing—whenever and wherever qualified people can cheat their inferiors out of the time it takes. Thank God you're getting it.

That is the longest excerpt. A shorter one, from a letter of February or March (he never dated his letters):

I'm in a bad period: incertitude and disintegration on almost every count. Somehow fed up and paralytic with the job; horribly bad sleeping rhythm; desperate need to live regularly & still more to do new work of my own; desperate knowledge that with all the time on earth I could as I spiritually feel now be capable of neither. . . . Alma is in Mexico—so is Joel—nominally, presumably, perhaps very probably, that is broken forever. And so far, I am not doing the one thing left me to do if it is ever possibly to reintegrate: entirely leave knowing Mia. It is constantly in the bottom of my gut—petrifying everything else—that I must, and will; and I still do nothing. A kind of bottomless sadness, impotence and misery in which one can neither move a hand nor keep it still without some further infliction on one or another. . . . For some doubtless discreditable reason it is of some good to speak of it, but I hope I don't do so at your expense, in sympathy or concern (I've known such things to derail me)—There is truly no need; as I say, I'm only too detached and anesthetized.

I delayed 2 months in all this trouble, in correcting proofs, but all is done now so I presume the machinery is turning. Don't yet know the publication date though.

Another one from about June, 1941:

Your last letters have sounded so thoroughly well in the head and health and so exciting in potentiality, that the thought of its shutting-off in a few more months, with your return to work, has made me probably almost as sick as it makes you.

I think this could be rather easily solved as follows:

What with one expense and another I shall nowhere near have paid off my debts by October and so will nowhere near be free to quit work and get to my own. So why don't I continue at this work and you continue at yours, for 6 months or 8 or a year (we can arrange that) during which I could send you and Eleanor $100 a month.

That would be very scrawny to live on most parts of this country; but apparently in Mexico would be: in Mexico City an adequate poverty; elsewhere an amplitude. This would, then, involve living where perhaps you might rather not; but a living, and free time, would be assured. And when I am able to quit work, if you are ready or need to come back, you could do likewise for me on some general equalization—

I think that by this or some such arrangement we & others might really get clear time when we are ripe for it, and it seems a better chance than any other—What do you think? . . .

Another a bit later:

Nothing on earth could make me feel worse than that you should for any reason whatever have to come back now that you are ripe for so much.

As for the money, I feel as you do, that it belongs to him who most needs it at a given time—your need for it for the next year or so is far out of proportion to any I could have short of a year or so of freedom first, and greater too than you would be likely to have again, without a long stretch of preparatory freedom. I think neither of us should think twice about your later paying me back—that is a wrong conception of the whole thing. I'll be able to take care of myself, one way or another, when my time comes for it—meanwhile I'll be best taking care for things I care for most, if I can make freedom and work possible for you when you can make best use of it.

I'm talking badly out of turn in all this walking-in and urging—I hope you can forgive it. It seems terribly crucial to me that you stay free at this particular time, and criminal if you don't. . . .

Chambers is still moving Books at *Time*—Stockley does Letters, and an occasional review. If you should come back—which God forbid—I imagine I could get switched to movies & you could replace me here.

13

I hope an occasional reader will understand that the foregoing private things are quoted after long hesitation and at the expense of my heart's blood. I think I am aware of every way in which they—and he, and I—can be taken advantage of. Jim Agee's agonies and his nobleness are equally the affair of no one who cannot keep still, or as good as still, about them, and there is no chance that all of you can. But some of you can, and some of you are thirty or thirty-one and hard beset and bound to someone in brotherhood, perhaps in art, and you may see that the brotherhood you know is of a kind really wider than you may have thought, binding others among the living and the dead. It is best, at any rate, that you should have the living movement of his own mind about his New York life and the dissolution of his second marriage, and it is essential that you should see proof of selflessness in a man who often appeared self-centered, and often was.

Before the publication of *Let Us Now Praise Famous Men,* just before I returned to New York, I received the book in September, 1941, for review in *Time.* When Jim got word of this he wrote at once, airmail special, to make sure whether I had been consulted, whether I had time to spare for it, and whether if, consulted or not, I did have time and would write the review, we shouldn't agree that he would not read it. I wrote a review but the editor who had invited it thought it was too stiff and reverent (he was right) and sent it back. He reviewed the book himself, recognized great writing in it, but classified it as "a distinguished failure." By this he, as an old *Fortune* editor, did not really mean that if *Fortune* had done it it would have been a success, but that was true: it would have been objective and clearly organized and readable and virtuously restrained, and would have sounded well and been of small importance beyond the month it appeared. A failure, on the contrary, it consciously was, a "young man's book," and a sinful book to boot (as Jim called it in a letter to Father Flye) and was thereby true to the magnitude and difficulty of the case including the observer. It is a classic, and perhaps the only classic, of the whole period, of the whole attempted *genre.* Photographs and text alike are bitten out by the very juices of the men who made them, and at the same time they have the piteous monumentality of the things and souls represented. Between them Agee and Evans made sure that George and Annie Mae Gudger are as immortal as Priam and Hecuba, and a lot closer to home.

I refused to take about a quarter of Jim's already mortgaged income, as he proposed, and returned to work for *Time* from October, 1941, to May, 1943, when to my relief I joined the navy. That October of my return he got "switched to movies," all right, and the last and perhaps the best phase of his life began. He and Mia Fritsch, who was to be his third wife, moved into the top-floor flat on Bleeker Street where they lived for the next ten years. Before I went to Fort Schuyler I managed to revise my manuscript of poems and put them together in a book, but not until Jim had commented on each in the most minute and delicate written criticism I ever had.

How more than appropriate, how momentous, it was, that after 1941 James Agee had "Cinema" for all occupation, could scarcely have been realized to the full by anyone, but a few of us at least felt uncommonly at peace about Jim's employment. He loved movies more than anyone I ever knew; he also lived them and thought them. To see and hear him describe a movie that he liked—shot by shot, almost frame by frame—was unquestionably better in many cases than to see the movie itself. Once when I was driving him across the Brooklyn Bridge in an open Model-A, he put on beside me such a rendering of Jimmy Cagney in a gangster film that I had to take my eyes off the road and give him my close attention. There must have been moments on that ride when we were both absolutely uninsurable.

He had wanted for years to do a scenario for Chaplin; whether he ever did more than imagine it, I have been unable to find out. By the late thirties he had, however, not only written but published two scenarios, both stunning exercises in what must be called screen-writing as literature. Both are published in this book.

The first, entitled "Notes for a Moving Picture: The House," was printed by Horace Gregory in a collection called *New Letters in America*, in 1937. Detailing ever shot and every sound, second by counted second, with his huge sensuous precision and scope, he constructed a screen fantasy for the camera, his angelic brain, before whose magnifying gaze or swimming movement a tall old house disclosed its ghastly, opulent moribundity until blown and flooded apart in an apocalyptic storm. Compare this with the efforts of more recently "rebellious" young men if you want to see how close to artistic nonexistence most of these are.

His second scenario was published in the first number of a review, *Films*, edited by Jay Leyda in

1939. In this one he merely (if you could use that word of anything Jim did) transposed into screen terms the famous scene in *Man's Fate* in which the hero, Kyo, waits with other Chinese Communists to be thrown by the Nationalists into the boiler of a locomotive. I am told that Malraux, who thought he had got everything out of this scene, thought again when he read the Agee script.

Concerning his movie reviewing for *Time,* T. S. Matthews has told me of one incident. Matthews as managing editor late one Sunday evening received and read a cover story Jim had written, on Laurence Olivier's *Hamlet,* and in Jim's presence indicated that he found it good enough, a little disappointing but good enough and in any case too late to revise; he initialed it for transmission to the printer (*Time* went to press on Monday) and in due course left for home presuming that Jim had also done so. At nine the next morning Jim presented him with a complete new handwritten version. Fully to appreciate this you would perhaps have to have felt the peculiar exhaustion of Sunday night at *Time.*

Jim Agee, however, had now found a kind of journalism answering to his passion. Beginning in December, 1942, he began the signed movie column for the *Nation,* every other week, that Margaret Marshall, the literary editor, invited and backed, and that in the next several years made him famous. He began to be called on at *Time* for general news stories to which no one else could do justice. Whatever he wrote for the magazine was so conspicuous that it might as well have been signed. In the Western Pacific I recognized at once his hand in *Time*'s page-one piece on the meaning of Hiroshima and Nagasaki:

> In what they said and did, men were still, as in the aftershock of a great wound, bemused and only semi-articulate, whether they were soldiers or scientists, or great statesmen, or the simplest of men. But in the dark depths of their minds and hearts, huge forms moved and silently arrayed themselves: Titans, arranging out

of the chaos an age in which victory was already only the shout of a child in the street.

. . . All thoughts and things were split. The sudden achievement of victory was a mercy, to the Japanese no less than to the United Nations; but mercy born of a ruthlessness beyond anything in human chronicle. The race had been won, the weapon had been used by those on whom civilization could best hope to depend; but the demonstration of power against living creatures instead of dead matter created a bottomless wound in the living conscience of the race. The rational mind had won the most Promethean of its conquests over nature, and had put into the hands of common man the fire and force of the sun itself. . . .

. . . The promise of good and of evil bordered alike on the infinite—with this further, terrible split in the fact: that upon a people already so nearly drowned in materialism even in peacetime, the good uses of this power might easily bring disaster as prodigious as the evil. The bomb rendered all decisions so far, at Yalta and at Potsdam, mere trivial dams across tributary rivulets. When the bomb split open the universe and revealed the prospect of the infinitely extraordinary, it also revealed the oldest, simplest, commonest, most neglected and most important of facts: that each man is eternally and above all else responsible for his own soul, and, in the terrible words of the Psalmist, that no man may deliver his brother, nor make agreement unto God for him.

Man's fate has forever been shaped between the hands of reason and spirit, now in collaboration, again in conflict. Now reason and spirit meet on final ground. If either or anything is to survive, they must find a way to create an indissoluble partnership.

Enough, and perhaps more than enough, has been said by various people about the waste of Jim's talents in journalism. It is a consolation and a credit to his employers that on this occasion, as on some others, he was invited and was able to dignify the reporting of events.

14

When I got back to New York in 1946 I found Jim in a corduroy jacket, a subtle novelty, and in a mood far more independent than before of Left or "Liberal" attitudes. He had become a trace more worldly and better off (I'm sure Matthews saw to it that he was decently paid) and more sure of himself; and high time, too. His years of hard living and testing and questioning had given him in his *Nation* articles a great charge of perceptions to express. His lifetime pleasure in cinema had made him a master of film craft and repertory. He had had some of the public recognition that he deserved. Most important of all, I think, this critical job had turned his mind a few compass points from the bearing Truth to the bearing Art. He was ready to take a hand, as he was soon to do, in the actual and practical making of films.

We were never estranged, but we were never so close again, either, as we had been before the war. The course of things for me (here I must intrude a little again) had not only broken up my own previous marriage and way of life but had brought me back in astonishment, with a terrific bump, into Catholic faith and practice; and though Jim intensely sympathized with me in the break-up, he regarded my conversion with careful reserve. He saw an old friend ravaged and transported by the hair into precisely the same system of coordinates that he had wrestled out of in the thirties. Or rather, not precisely the same. For in my turn I had reservations, now, about the quality of his old vision. It struck me that for him it must have been a matter of imagination and empathy, a profound and sacramental sense of the natural world, but only a notion of the incommensurable overhead, the change of light and being that leaves a man no fulcrum by which to dislodge himself from his new place. With my all-too-negative capability and other flaws, I could easily have been self-deceived, as he must have imagined. I was not, however. At any rate, I now wanted to lead a kind of life that Jim had rejected and, in his own and general opinion, outgrown; and there was (at most) one art that I might practice, the art of verse that he had likewise left behind.

All the same, the memory of what he had aspired literally to be, in college and for the first years thereafter, could return now and again to trouble him. One day in 1947 when he and Mia brought their first baby, Teresa, to spend an afternoon with my wife and myself, he handed me the two very sad and strange sonnets on the buried steed, published three years later in *Botteghe Oscure* and now included in the collection of Agee's poems recently edited by myself. His hand at verse had barely retained but not refined its skill, and there is a coarseness along with the complexity of these and other late sonnets. Two or three of the final poems are very beautiful, though. "Sleep, Child" certainly is, and so is the peerless Christmas ballad in Tennessee dialect (but I am not sure how late that one is, and have no clue as to when it was written).

The last verses that he wrote were some rather casually attempted drafts, by invitation, for a musical that in the late winter and spring of 1955 Lillian Hellman and Leonard Bernstein were trying to make of *Candide*. Both playwright and composer felt that these drafts wouldn't do, but Miss Hellman is not sure that Jim, who was more desperately ill than he knew, understood this before his fatal heart attack on May 16th. "He was not a lyric writer," Miss Hellman says. "Good poets often aren't." At my distance I find the episode fairly astringent. In their most nearly completed state, the drafts appear in Agee's *Collected Poems* at the end of Part IV. They may be compared with the lighter lyrics by various hands, mainly Richard Wilbur's, for the show as produced in December, 1956.

Helen Levitt has told me that only a year or so before his death in 1955 Jim seriously said to her that poetry had been his true vocation, the thing he was born to do, but that it was too difficult; on the other hand, work in films was pure pleasure for him. I think he had in mind the difficulty for everyone—not only for himself—of making true poetry in that time; I think, too, that what he was born to do, he did.

Jim's leaning to self-accusation does not seem to me very deplorable, however. It was, rather, part of what gave him his largeness among his contemporaries, most of whom were engaged in pretending that they were wonderful and their mishaps or shortcomings all ascribable to Society or History or Mother or other powers in the mythology of the period. I gather that he got cooler and tougher about everything in his last years, in particular about love. Before he went to the Coast, in the late forties, he wrote a draft scenario, never worked up for production or publication, in which with disabused and cruel objectivity he turned a camera eye on himself in his relations with women.

After my wife and I moved away from New York in the summer of 1949, we saw him only once again, for an evening, in the following spring. His last letter to me was from Malibu Beach in 1952: I had written to say how much I liked *The African Queen.* Of his final years I can have little to say. (I had been in Italy for two years when the shocking cable came to tell me of his death.) I am told that young men in New York began heroizing him and hanging on his words, but late one night at a *Partisan Review* sort of party a younger writer in impatience saw him as "a whisky-listless and excessive saint," I myself felt my heart sink when I began to read *The Morning Watch;* the writing seemed to me a little showy, though certainly with much to show; and I wondered if he were losing his irony and edge. It is pretty clear to me now that he had to go to those lengths of artifice and musical elaboration simply to make the break with journalism decisive. He never lost his edge, as *A Death in the Family* was to demonstrate—that narrative held so steadily and clearly in the middle distance and at the same time so full of Jim's power of realization, a contained power, fully comparable to that in the early work of Joyce. Let the easy remark die on your lips. Jim arrived at his austere style fifty years and a torn world away from Edwardian Dublin and Trieste; if it took him twenty years longer than it took Joyce, who else arrived at all?

The comparison with Joyce is worth pausing over a moment more. Each with his versatile and musical gift, each proud and a world-plunderer, each choosing the savage beauty of things as they are over the impossible pieties of adolescence, each concerned with the "conscience of his race." Agee had less ice-cold intellect; he could not have derived what Joyce did from Aquinas. He had, of course, nothing like Joyce's linguistic range. His affections were more widely distributed and perhaps dissipated. He inherited the violence that Americans inherit: a violence, too (it will not have escaped you), no more directed against office buildings, employers, and bourgeois horrors than against himself. The cinema that interested Joyce in its infancy had by Agee's time become a splendid art form, a successor perhaps to the art of fiction, and who else understood it better than he? The record is there in two volumes. Joyce had more irony, but Joyce, too, sentimentalized or angelicized the role of the artist. In all Agee's work the worst example of this is in the scenario of *Noa Noa,* and anyone can see that script becoming at times a maudlin caricature of the artist-as-saint.

Jim's weakness and strength were not so easy to tell apart. Consider, if you will, his early story, "They That Sow in Sorrow Shall Reap." Through weakness, through not being able to do otherwise, the boy narrator brings the laborer to the boardinghouse and so precipitates the catastrophe that leaves the scene and people in ruins. Or is it entirely through weakness? Is it not also through a dispassionate willingness to see his microcosm convulsed for the pure revelation of it, for an epiphany that he may record? Was it weakness later that kept James Agee at *Fortune,* or was it strategy and will, for the sake of the great use he would make of it? Ruins were left behind then, too, but in New York journalism of the thirties no one created anything like the Alabama book. Likewise, no weekly reviewer of the forties created anything like the body of new insights contained in his *Nation* film pieces. Again, no writer of film pieces prepared himself to write for cinema with such clean and lovely inventiveness (barring the instance I have noted). Finally, no scriptwriter except possibly Faulkner exercised, or learned, in film writing the control over fiction that went into *A Death in the Family*. When you reflect on his life in this way, weakness and strategy, instinct and destiny seem all one thing.

In one of the best novels of the sixties, a charmer by a southerner, I find a sentence running like this, of cemeteries that at first look like cities from a train passing at a slight elevation: ". . . tiny streets and corners and curbs and even plots of lawn, all of such a proportion that in the very instant of being mistaken and from the eye's own necessity, they set themselves off into the distance like a city seen from far away." * It is an Agee sentence, so I conclude that his writing has entered into the mainstream of English. But I share with him a disinclination for Literary History and its idiom. Jim may be a Figure for somebody else; he cannot be one for me. "This breathing joy, heavy on us all"—it is his no longer; nevertheless, I have written this in his presence and therefore as truly as I could. Quite contrary to what has been said about him, he amply fulfilled his promise. In one of his first sonnets he said, of his kin, his people:

'Tis mine to touch with deathlessness their clay,
And I shall fail, and join those I betray.

In respect to that commission, who thinks that there was any failure or betrayal?

*From *The Moviegoer*, by Walker Percy.

The Turning Point

David McDowell

WHEN I FIRST met Agee in mid-April of 1936, I was eighteen and on the verge of graduating from Saint Andrew's School in Tennessee. I felt I already knew him, for he was the "Rufus" I had heard so much about since I was thirteen—from members of the faculty and staff of Saint Andrew's, but most of all from Father and Mrs. Flye, his dearest friends and mentors. I could not get used to calling him "Jim" until 1948 when I had returned to this country after the war. By that time, even Father Flye had given up on anything but "Jim" (though Agee's mother spoke of him as Rufus until her death in 1966).

I knew that lovely spring was a turning point for me, but it was many years before I realized what changes were in the offing for Jim. He was twenty-six years old, trim, tanned and vigorously handsome. He and his wife Via had just driven up from Anna Maria, an island off the west coast of Florida, where they had spent a six months' leave of absence. It had been his first real break from New York City since he had joined *Fortune* right after his graduation from Harvard in 1932. It had been a relaxed time of writing, reading, tennis, and swimming. He was never again to have so long a respite from work and pressure.

It was also Jim's first visit back to Sewanee Mountain since he had left Saint Andrew's in 1924 at the age of eleven. He and Via stayed with the Flyes in their cottage on the school grounds for a little over a month. Later in June he wrote Father Flye. "I agree with Mrs. Flye: no time or visit ever, anywhere, has been so good and meant so much to me. Much love to you both."

2

That time of year on the mountain offers beauty beyond compare. This is no place to dwell upon it, but I wish I could quote the whole chapter on Sewanee in William Alexander Percy's *Lanterns on the Levee*—a book perhaps then already in the writing, though it wasn't published until 1941. (Jim wrote a review of it for *Time*—if memory serves—and I remember his reading to me, in the summer of 1942, the sections on mountain woods and flowers.)

So it was a time and season that he remembered and reveled in, and as Father Flye had classes and papers to grade, Jim and I often walked the woods or the winding paths. He especially wanted to retrace his steps to Sand Cut, an abandoned sand quarry now, as then, deep and filled with water. He made no mention of it in any literary way, but I am sure he was touching base with some of the memories and perceptions that would later be used so well in *The Morning Watch.*

We also walked out to the cliff at Piney Point, passing the cottage his mother and his sister Emma had lived in while he was a student at Saint Andrew's. He made no comment, and, as I remember, spoke little on these outings, except to respond to my talk about poetry or to marvel at how little things had changed. Many friends have written about what a brilliant talker Agee was, but only rarely has anyone pointed out what an incredibly sensitive and perceptive listener he was. Perhaps Louis Kronenberger came closest in his brief but beautiful memorial tribute to Agee in *FYI,* Time, Inc.'s house organ:

> No one else I can think of absorbed so much from all he encountered—or related so much in encountering it.

No one else I ever knew so quickly got the point or sensed the purport of what you were saying: with Jim, you almost literally never needed to finish a sentence.

Jim and I also talked a lot about the beautiful and intelligent girl I was in love with—the first great love of my life. Agee wanted to hear all about her and to meet her, which was easy, since she lived only two miles away in Sewanee and had her own car. So one Saturday afternoon, she came out and picked us up, and we drove all over the mountain top. Somehow Via did not come along, but she and Jim later became almost as taken as I was with that lovely creature.

During those weeks Jim was relaxed and in constant good spirits. He was completely at ease with himself and quite obviously happy to be back on his beloved mountain, which was still almost as isolated as it had been in his childhood. As Will Percy wrote in *Lanterns on the Levee:*

> It's a long way away, even from Chattanooga, in the middle of woods, on top of a bastion of mountains crenelated with blue coves. It is so beautiful that people who have once been there always, one way or another, come back. For such as can detect apple green in an evening sky, it is Arcadia—not the one that never used to be, but the one that many people always live in; only this one can be shared.

Jim once said to me—perhaps at Piney Point—that this was his favorite part of the world (it *still* is mine), and in the years we were both living in New York City, we often spoke of our mutual longing for it.

He was also probably in as good shape as he had ever been. The school's tennis court was about twenty yards behind Father Flye's house, and as tennis was not then a particularly popular sport at the school, it was usually empty. So we played fiercely almost every day. I usually won, but it wasn't easy, for Jim was both tireless and highly competitive. I was never again to see him so merry and serene, or so healthy.

3

But I want to get back to poetry, for at that time it was the main concern of us both. On Anna Maria he had been working mostly on poetry, although he mentioned some autobiographical material about his childhood in Knoxville to Father Flye, and Fitzgerald quotes from a journal, "Have been working (c. 12–15,000 words) on the footloose in Knoxville idea. Don't know." We don't know either exactly what prose he wrote during those months in Florida, but his father's death haunted him. His mother told me that as early as his final years at Exeter he had told her that he wanted to write about that early death and its effects on those most close to him. So, the genesis of *A Death in the Family,* whose central theme is the death of a young father of two small children, actually came some years before Agee started writing it.

We know much more about the poetry he was writing and which poems were later published, but we don't know how much of the "Knoxville idea" material was included in *A Death in the Family.* It seems likely that some of it was, because we do know that "Knoxville: Summer 1915" was written on Anna Maria, for Jim read it to Father and Mrs. Flye shortly after his arrival at Saint Andrew's. As I wrote in the editorial note to *A Death in the Family* in 1957: "The short section 'Knoxville: Summer 1915,' which serves as a sort of prologue, has been added. It was not a part of the manuscript Agee left, but the editors would certainly have urged him to include it in the final draft." To be sure, it is not "poetry," but it contains more than most of the published poetry of the decade. At the 1972 Saint Andrew's dedicatory symposium on Agee's work, Walker Percy remarked that Agee "brought back poetry into modern prose." The other panelists agreed.

During our talks, Jim made no mention of any prose at all. He read me some poems, and he showed me three or four he had written, but he showed more interest in the poetry I had been writing. For a couple of years, Father Flye had sent him from time to time some of my work, and I want to quote from one of Jim's replies. It contains good advice to young writers and kind encouragement. Agee's generosity was legendary.

David's poem is likable and moving as the first poems of Keats are to me—whether there's any such parallel in talent I don't know but only reasonably doubt. Which is vulgar, ridiculous & uncalled for but I do care not only that he should want to and enjoy continuing to write but for the writing as such. On that, excuse a few half-ideas. Most of the language and a good deal of the thought and feeling of the poetry is very naturally "literary"—which is the way & about the proportion it comes to nine out of ten writers bad or good or for that matter great, to start with—and from which Lord knows there is a lot to be learned. But also a great deal of harm to be absorbed which can be hard & even impossible to clear the head of. I was going to say I hope he can be talked with & shown the various & more important (in fact indispensable) other contents of poetry & of writing. But that is really stupid: except for certain & small pieces of help, those are either learned by yourself or not learned. But it has all caused me plenty of trouble, and is still doing that. My wish would be to save anyone else of it: but each person can only save himself: I shouldn't have mentioned it. I'm glad of this possibility of his coming to Yale: God knows he deserves it. No. Excuse my opinion which is both callow & only personal: he deserves everything which can open clear & sharpen his appetite and feed it, and I don't know at all that that is best to be had at Yale or Harvard though at such places it does exist in concentrated as well as disguised forms. I'm not such a dope as to think I or anyone can find his own way unassisted but the more of that and the less guidance & elaboration of the means, the better. College elaborated a lot of things out of recognition for me and that was partly my limitations, immaturity, etc. Thinking of it now I would give anything to have had access to a good library and perhaps also to lectures, and to friends & acquaintances of all sorts & to have let it go at that. But that's wishful and probably romanticized feeling. Probably I'd have thought no more clearly and used time no better than I did. And do. Phooey. I really deserve to have no opinions. But I wish only best luck to David, whatever that may mean or be, and will you give him my best. . . .

As Robert Fitzgerald and others have lamented, Agee's poems were too little known, then and now. After 1936, he wrote less and less poetry, for he was at the great turning point of his life. He was to be tied up almost entirely with prose. At Saint Andrew's he was unaware that on his return to New York he would be handed his most important assignment. He got back to *Fortune* in late May, and he wrote Father Flye on June 18th:

I must cut this short and do a week's work in next twenty hours or so: have been assigned to do a story on: a sharecropper family (daily & yearly life): and also a study of Farm Economics in the South (impossible for me): and also on the several efforts to help the situation: i.e. Govt. and state work; theories & wishes of Southern liberals; whole story of the 2 Southern Unions. Best break I ever had on *Fortune.* Feel terrific personal responsibility toward story; considerable doubts of my ability to bring it off; considerable more of *Fortune's* ultimate willingness to use it as it seems (in theory) to me. Will be starting South Saturday. For a month's work. . . .

Agee and Walker Evans spent July and August in Alabama living with three tenant families. Agee was preoccupied for the next four years with what became *Let Us Now Praise Famous Men,* then with film criticism and scripts, *The Morning Watch,* and *A Death in the Family.*

4

The school year was running out. Like all such times it was hectic, and the last week or so I saw less and less of Jim. However, he and Via did go to the commencement dance with my girl and me, and we all had a great time. It was the only time I ever saw Jim dance. He had gone south without a suit or tie, and as we were about the same size, I lent him one of mine. He put it to good use, wearing it to a faculty literary club in Sewanee and to the commencement ceremonies which were held a week after the dance.

My clearest memory of him and of that important time in my life has to do with a speech. I had to give a valedictory address. I had written what I wanted to say on that somewhat sad occasion, but I could not seem to find a satisfactory way to begin. After lunch on the day before commencement, in desperation, I went down to Father Flye's house to seek his help. He and Jim were talking in the living room. I explained my predicament, and as my speech was not long, I asked Father Flye to read it. When he finished, he said he would have to think about it some but that it would have to wait until after a faculty meeting he had to attend in a few minutes. As he got ready to leave, Jim asked if he could read it. Of course Father Flye and I were delighted.

Father Flye had left before Jim finished reading it. He leafed through it again quickly. Then he said, "I think I have an idea. I'll be back in a minute or so," and he disappeared into Father Flye's study which adjoined the room we were in.

A half hour passed, then an hour; and I grew more and more nervous, thinking that Jim was finding the whole thing impossible or that it had put him asleep on the couch in the study. I was on the brink of fleeing to escape disgrace, after over an hour and a half had gone by, when Jim came out and handed me a couple of sentences in his miniscule script. "How do you think this will work as a lead?" he asked. *Lead* was a new word to me, but in that context I knew what it meant. Here is what he wrote: "Before another hour has passed, we of the senior class will no longer be students at Saint Andrew's. We shall have been advanced into a world new to us, and not yet, clearly known to us."

I felt then—and still do—how clear, how simple, how appropriate to that occasion. But I thought, even more, of his generosity and his total *engagement* in everything he did.

I do not expect to see his like again.

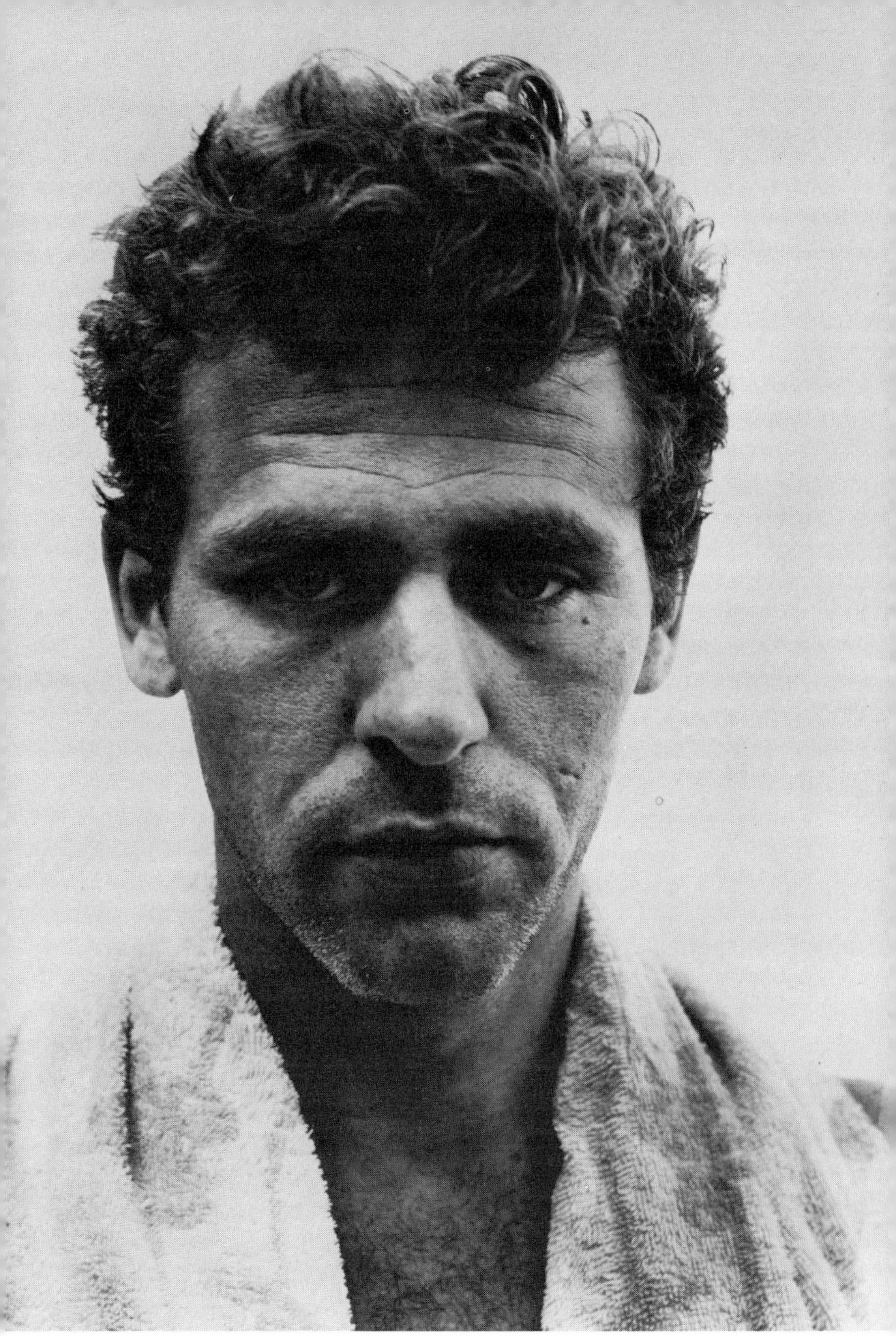

James Agee in 1936

Walker Evans

AT THE TIME, Agee was a youthful-looking twenty-seven. I think he felt he was elaborately masked, but what you saw right away—alas for conspiracy—was a faint rubbing of Harvard and Exeter, a hint of family gentility, and a trace of romantic idealism. He could be taken for a likable American young man, an above-average product of the Great Democracy from any part of the country. He didn't look much like a poet, an intellectual, an artist, or a Christian, each of which he was. Nor was there outward sign of his paralyzing, self-lacerating anger. His voice was pronouncedly quiet and low pitched, though not of "cultivated" tone. It gave the impression of diffidence, but never of weakness. His accent was more or less unplaceable and it was somewhat variable. For instance, in Alabama it veered toward country-southern, and I may say he got away with this to the farm families and to himself.

His clothes were deliberately cheap, not only because he was poor but because he wanted to be able to forget them. He would work a suit into fitting him perfectly by the simple method of not taking it off much. In due time the cloth would mold itself to his frame. Cleaning and pressing would have undone this beautiful process. I exaggerate, but it did seem sometimes that wind, rain, work, and mockery were his tailors. On another score, he felt that wearing good, expensive clothes involved him in some sort of claim to superiority of the social kind. Here he occasionally confused his purpose, and fell over into a knowingly comical inverted dandyism. He got more delight out of factory-seconds sneakers and a sleazy cap than a straight dandy does from waxed calf Peal shoes and a brushed Lock & Co. bowler.

Physically Agee was quite powerful, in the deceptive way of uninsistent large men. In movement he was rather graceless. His hands were large, long, bony, light, and uncared for. His gestures were one of the memorable things about him. He seemed to model, fight, and stroke his phrases as he talked. The talk, in the end, was his great distinguishing feature. He talked his prose, Agee prose. It was hardly a twentieth-century style; it had Elizabethan colors. Yet it had extraordinarily knowledgeable contemporary content. It rolled just as it reads; but he made it sound natural—something just there in the air like any other part of the world. How he did this no one knows. You would have blinked, gaped, and very likely run from this same talk delivered without his mysterious ability. It wasn't a matter of show, and it wasn't necessarily bottle-inspired. Sheer energy of imagination was what lay behind it. This he matched with physical energy. Many a man or woman has fallen exhausted to sleep at four in the morning bang in the middle of a remarkable Agee performance, and later learned that the man had continued it somewhere else until six. Like many born writers who are floating in the illusory amplitude of their youth, Agee did a great deal of writing in the air. Often you had the impulse to gag him and tie a pen to his hand. That wasn't necessary; he was an exception among talking writers. He wrote—devotedly and incessantly.

Night was his time. In Alabama he worked I don't know how late. Some parts of *Let Us Now Praise Famous Men* read as though they were written on the spot at night. Later, in a small house in Frenchtown, New Jersey, the work, I think, was largely night-written. Literally the result shows this; some of the sections read best at night, far in the night. The first passage of "A Country Letter" (p. 49), is particularly night-permeated.

Agee worked in what looked like a rush and a rage. In Alabama he was possessed with the business, jamming it all into the days and the nights. He must not have slept. He was driven to see all he could of the families' day, starting, of course, at dawn. In one way, conditions there were ideal. He could live inside the subject, with no distractions. Back-country poor life wasn't really far from him, actually. He had some of it in his blood, through relatives in Tennessee. Anyway, he was in flight from New York magazine editorial offices, from Greenwich Village social-intellectual evenings, and especially from the whole world of high-minded, well-bred, money-hued culture, whether authoritarian or libertarian. In Alabama he sweated and scratched with submerged glee. The families understood what he was down there to do. He'd explained it, in such a way that they were interested in *his* work. He wasn't playing. That is why in the end he left out certain completed passages that were entertaining, in an acid way. One of these was a long, gradually hilarious aside on the subject of hens. It was a virtuoso piece heightened with allegory and bemused with the pathetic fallacy.

He won almost everybody in those families—perhaps too much—even though some of the individuals were hardbitten, sore, and shrewd. Probably it was his diffidence that took him into them. That nonassurance was, I think, a hostage to his very Anglican childhood training. His Christianity—if an outsider may try to speak of it—was a punctured and residual remnant, but it was still a naked, root emotion. It was an ex-Church, or non-Church matter, and it was hardly in evidence. All you saw of it was an ingrained courtesy, an uncourtly courtesy that emanated from him toward everyone, perhaps excepting the smugly rich, the pretentiously genteel, and the police. After a while, in a round-about way, you discovered that, to him, human beings were at least possibly immortal and literally sacred souls.

The days with the families came abruptly to an end. Their real content and meaning has all been shown. The writing they induced is, among other things, the reflection of one resolute, private rebellion. Agee's rebellion was unquenchable, self-damaging, deeply principled, infinitely costly, and ultimately priceless.

A Real Bohemian

Louis Kronenberger

RELATIVELY FEW PEOPLE are altogether easy to share an office with; Jim was an ideal one. Partly from having been brought up in the South, but preeminently from having the most delicate sensibilities; he was the most courteous of men. He had equally sensibilities of thought as of feeling; you had only to start a sentence to find him anticipating the rest of it. In the office, as I remember, we seldom stopped working to talk at length; but we traded comic items and literary tidbits back and forth, and every so often, late in the afternoon, we would go out for a drink. These proved to be extremely pleasant sessions but dangerously protracted ones which I would eventually have to call time on, even so arriving home more tardy, if possible, than tipsy. Jim's losing all sense of time was, in my experience, his only failure of "thoughtfulness" and of course not that at all; it came about through his love of talk, often involving the pursuit of ideas, and it constituted a facet of his essential bohemianism. He was a real bohemian, beginning with how he wanted to live, which was in no particular way; but far from any element of conformity, there was no apparent element of rebelliousness. He seemed adaptable to almost any situation, this not so much because nothing human was alien to him as that almost everything human was interesting. He was a steady and heroic drinker, though on "social" lines; never really unsteady so long as he was seated and went on talking away with great verve or intensity, gesturing in great wide arcs of space, and drinking, it sometimes seemed as unawarely as breathing, in great easy draughts. The only trouble—and it became a subject of humorous despair for the friends whose houses he went to—was that 2 A.M. or 3 A.M. or 4 A.M. might come, and Jim show not the slightest inclination to go home. This, should you have a seven months' pregnant wife, or have to be up by seven o'clock, or, as the host, just not be able to keep awake, might have its inconvenient side. Then, suddenly penetrating the haze that never muddled his eloquence, Jim would become aware that it might be awfully late; and he would stand himself up, lunge contritely forward and somehow, ceremoniously apologetic, take his leave.

Dinner at the Agees'—which was on the fifth and top floor of an old building in the Village—had about it a kind of charming unpunctual punctilio, an engaging, unthought-out yet thoughtful, hospitality. Mia, Jim's Austrian-born wife, was a calm-mannered likable woman and a very good cook; and dinner, equally for how good it tasted and how festively it was consumed, was a very pleasant meal. It might be preceded, during an hour or more of drinking, by a need for milk or bread or bottled goods, with Jim possibly dashing twice down four flights of steep stairs and then up them—a routine matter it would seem, and no doubt straining the heart condition which he knew about and seemed to dismiss, and from which he died. At dinner, drinking wine with the rest of us, might be an Agee four-year-old in a high chair; and toward the end of dinner, there was perhaps another dash downstairs for cigarettes. It was all of a piece, all a pleasure, and somehow rather memorable.

Having achieved by his movie criticism in *Time,* and even more in the *Nation,* a great recognition and prestige that reverberated in Hollywood, Jim, somewhere around 1950 resigned from *Time* to go there; but he continued to write periodically for *Life.*

The last time that I saw him he stuck his head through my office door, suggesting a drink, and we had a longish session in which he talked of movies he had been asked to write and of others he wanted to. Hollywood, I gather, used him rather badly,

which was perhaps foreseeable, since Jim simply disregarded not only money but the protective clauses of modern business life. He had even ignored the insurance arrangement available to Time-Incers. Of the people I have known he was one of the few who truly had something large, open, magnetic about them, and a touch—but no Midas touch—of genius.

This doesn't mean that he lacked faults or weaknesses; they, indeed, are implicit in the legend that he hastily became. Something demonic, or priapic, or reckless, or mysterious, or doomed would seem to be a necessary ingredient of such legendry, from Marlowe to Shelley and Byron, from Rimbaud to Baron Corvo and Jack London and, contemporary with Jim, Dylan Thomas. The legend of course is never really the man and indeed often misrepresents him. I never knew Jim well enough, and I am not psychologist enough, to feel I could even tentatively provide a portrait. His "life," though unimportant beside his personality and his work, had its standard ingredients of legend-making: there were wine and women in it, and moments of rage, and others that suggested bravura; but the first two things fit the sense of physical size he imparted, and the personal magnetism; and the last two are less significant in themselves than indicating, in a greatly gifted man of gentleness and courtesy, the "required" intensity. What perhaps, in the man one knew, provided a resonant inner voice and an added dimension was Jim's religious nature, which ran very deep in him. His rage seemed a kind of denial of rancor—something heated and impassioned, not petty. He had magnanimity but not, I think, strength. There was something—though there is perhaps a better word—weak about him, partly owing perhaps to his physical endowments, which must have seemed inexhaustible, as must also have seemed his talents. The something weak was not something flabby, but just not sufficiently firm. In the man, and from a desire to seize on all experience, it perhaps derived from a kind of scorn of something so middle class as willpower. In the writer, with gifts evocative of genius, there was seldom the exacting judgment and long-range control to produce a great work; what emerged were great passages. Jim had considerable control and judgment, but nothing to cope with the swell of language, the onrush of imagination in his writing;

as well try to filter a waterfall. The filter and the file are what his work most needed. There was a much less costly element of this in Jim's talk. Now and then toward the end of a session I found myself bored from a sense of excess, repetitiousness, undirected intensity in what he said. Much of this is, of course, part of many legends; legends, as a matter of fact, don't grow up around men of logical thought and disciplined action. Nor can one be both religious and rational by nature, or in one's encounter with life both immensely responsive, and restrained. Each way of life sets *faults* in opposition as well, and Jim's way had no touch of expediency, calculation, self-serving forethought.

For FYI, *Time*'s in-house publication, Louis Kronenberger wrote the following memorial:

You did not need to know Jim Agee personally to grasp how marvelously special he was. His signature was upon everything he wrote, whether critical or creative, books or movies, prose or poetry. There was a richness and, in the words of Keats, a 'fine excess' about it; an imagination furnished out with miraculously right words. In his movie criticism there are countless examples of Jim's ability to penetrate, encompass, and above all enlarge his subject. In his creative writing there are passages that—quite simply—it took genius to write, but that not even genius could have written without an accompanying largeness of heart and mind.

But those who did personally know Jim knew what was incalculably greater. I don't mean only the charm, the humor, the sweetness, the passionate aliveness. He was one of the very few—they are really painfully few—men of great gifts who are even more distinguished as human beings. Jim saved nothing of himself for his writing—all the sympathy, generosity, nobility of feeling that beat through his words shone equally in his actions. He lived his gifts; and if this was at a certain cost in concrete achievement, living them as he did was a far rarer achievement. No one else I can think of absorbed so much from all he encountered—or released so much in encountering it. No one else I ever knew so quickly got the point or sensed the purport of what you were saying: with Jim, you almost literally never needed to finish a sentence. As for his place here, he was *Time*'s finest writer, and will remain one of its most beautiful memories.

Agee at *Time*

T. S. Matthews

IF YOU'VE PLAYED tennis all your life, you can get a pretty fair idea of a man's character after half a dozen sets of singles with him. By the same token, you can get to know a man by working alongside him. Perhaps you don't know him as well as if you had often sat up all night drinking together, or as if you were both survivors in the same open boat after a disaster at sea; all the same, if you work with a man you will read him—not like a book, perhaps, but at least like its chapter headings.

It was by working with Agee on *Time* that I got to know him. We had a few friends in common; I remember seeing him at a Greenwich Village party; and once I paid him a visit when he was in the hospital after an operation—for appendicitis, I think. But most of our meetings took place at the office and were strictly business: he was a *Time* writer (mainly of cinema reviews) and I was his editor.

There was no one at all like Agee on the *Time* staff, although there were some others who were also out of the ordinary, and who behaved as if they had a special license. Agee's office-mate, Whittaker Chambers, was one of these. Physically and temperamentally they could not have been more unlike, and politically they were at right angles, but they shared a preference for working at night, and this habit led first to a mutually tolerant acquaintance and then to a warm friendship.

Many years later, recalling those days, and with

Agee and Chambers (and one or two others) in mind, I tried to characterize these difficult individuals—difficult, that is to say, from a managing editor's point of view. I wrote:

> I learned to value the steady man, the slogger, the writer who got his copy in on time and did what he said he would. If it had not been for him and his kind, we should never have got to press. I often thanked God for him. But my real Te Deums were reserved for the uncertain performance of his unsteady brother. There were never more than three or four (out of fifty-odd) of this breed on the staff, and I suppose that was about as many as we could safely carry. In many cases, they were 'hard to work with'—touchy, suspicious, arrogant, unpredictable. Their working habits were spectacularly individual. When they worked, they often worked all night, then disappeared for indeterminate periods. They were not only subject to temperamental tantrums but prey to fits of despair; and they had absolutely no feeling about going to press, one way or the other. They sometimes missed the target completely, or failed to pull the trigger. But when they did make a hit, it was often a bull's eye. They were regarded by the rest of the staff with mingled contempt and awe. I loved and cherished them. They were the seagreen incorruptibles who acknowledged no authority but some inner light of their own. These rarities were in journalism but never altogether of it. They gave their editors more trouble than anybody but they made the whole undertaking worthwhile.

I had two episodes in mind, as I wrote of Agee the journalist. Once, on his own hook, after a week of working late nights, he stayed up all night and completely rewrote a "cover story," a long review of Olivier's film of *Hamlet,* because he thought I was a little disappointed in his original version. And I was, a little: it was well above *Time*'s standard but not quite up to Agee's. Nevertheless a respectable piece of work, and he was so late getting it in that there was no time to make more than minor changes. All I could do about his revised version was thank him and try to explain that there simply wasn't time now to get the story retyped, let alone set.

When people tell me about "*Time* style" or assert that *Time* has always written in some form of pidgin English, I remember Agee, and the editorial he wrote on the atomic bomb, just after we had dropped it on Nagasaki and Hiroshima. "When the bomb split open the universe and revealed the prospect of the infinitely extraordinary, it also revealed the oldest, simplest, commonest, most neglected and most important of facts: that each man is eternally and above all else responsible for his soul, and, in the terrible words of the Psalmist, that no man may deliver his brother, nor make agreement unto God for him."

I have to say that though I admired and respected Agee, he does not play the hero's part in all the scenes I remember: not all are good and some are ambiguous. When he came to see me about a leave of absence I urged him to cut loose and resign, telling him that if he had to come back to *Time* he could always be sure of getting his job again. I hoped he would go off to some quiet spot and write whatever he felt he had to write. Instead he did a couple of pieces for *Life,* and then went to Hollywood to work with John Huston, of all halfway people.

I knew or suspected that he had a violent temper; all the same, it was a shock when I picked up my office telephone one night and by some accident of crossed wires overheard Agee, his voice thick with drink and anger, cursing the telephone operator as if he hated and despised her. And I learned with an equal shock, this time of relief, that his knocking down a girl at a *Time* party was an accident: I was afraid that it had been an act of drunken rage.

And there were questions to which I never knew an adequate answer: why did he leave so much of his own work unfinished, partly finished or not even begun? Why, after quitting *Time*—and none too soon—did he waste his substance on Hollywood movies? Why didn't he get his teeth fixed, and smoke and

drink less; did he *want* his life cut short?

But all such questions and doubts are of no account in the light of what he saw, what he was, and what he tried to do. He saw something sacred in the hopeless poor. He was "human": that is to say, contradictory and unworthy of himself. By the seriousness of his intention, a seriousness that pervades his writing as veins and arteries branch through a body, he makes us feel like the liars we are.

Perhaps he was torn apart by all the different things he was or might have been: an intellectual, a poet, a cineaste, a revolutionary, God's fool. A wild yearning violence beat in his blood, certainly, and just as certainly the steadier pulse of a saint. He wanted to destroy with his own hands everything in the world, including himself, that was shoddy, false and despicable; and to worship God, who made all things.

Jim Agee, A Memoir

Dwight Macdonald

IN THE TWENTIES, James Agee and I both attended Phillips Exeter Academy, which then had an extraordinary English department: Myron Williams, E. S. W. Kerr, Hank Couse, Dr. Cushwa, James Plaisted ("Cokey Joe") Webber, to set down the names of those who taught us something about writing. Jim and I just missed each other at Exeter, I graduating in the spring of 1924 and he arriving there in the fall of 1925. I find I wrote an old Exeter friend, Dinsmore Wheeler, in 1929, apropos of a project for starting an intellectual community on his farm in Ohio: "Our generation is one of great power, I think. There's talent running around like loose quicksilver. A fellow named Jim Agee, one-time editor of the P.E.A. *Monthly,* has The Stuff. I've never met him but I've corresponded with him. He is all there when it comes to creative writing, or rather *will be* all there."

Agee was then at Harvard and I on *Fortune* and we kept on corresponding, mostly about movies, which interested us as a form of self-expression much more than writing did. "A fellow in my dormitory," he wrote me that year, "owns a movie camera (not the kind you set buzzing and jam into the diaphragm) and has done some interesting work with it. . . . It's possible we'll do two movies [a documentary on Boston and a film version of a short story he had written]. The idea is that I'll devise shots, angles, camera work, etc., and stories; he'll take care of the photography and lighting." (Like my own dream of an Ohio Brook

Farm, neither of these projects seems to have come to anything.) We both admired the standard things—Griffith, Chaplin, Stroheim, the Russians, the Germans—despised the big American productions ("*Noah's Ark* is the worst and most pretentious movie ever made," he wrote.) and looked desperately for signs of life in Hollywood: "Saw a movie today, *Hearts in Dixie* was its unfortunate title. The thing itself struck me as pretty swell [though] there was no camera work and very little else to recommend it from the real director's point of view." His enthusiasm seems to have been based mostly on the fact it was less melodramatic than *Porgy*. Similarly, his "Ever noticed Dorothy Mackaill? Along the general lines of Esther Ralston" was intended as a compliment. We really were hopeful then.

"I'm going to spend the summer working in the wheatfields, starting in Oklahoma in June," he wrote May 10, 1929. "The thing looks good in every way. I like to get drunk and will; I like to sing and learn dirty songs and hobo ones—and will; I like to be on my own—the farther from home the better—and will; and I like the heterogeneous gang that moves north on the job. . . . Also I like bumming. . . . Finally, I like saving money, and this promises from $5 to $7 a day." That summer I got a pencil-scrawled note dated "Oshkosh, Neb., maybe August 1" (the postmark is August 5):

Dear Dwight—

If pen and ink and white paper gave you trouble, this should rival the Rosetta stone. To add insult to injury, it's written in a wagon-bed—about my only chance to write is between loads.

Am now working at hauling and scooping grain on a "combine" crew. . . . Kansas is the most utterly lousy state I've ever seen. Hot as hell and trees ten miles apart. I worked near a town which proudly bore the name "Glade" because of a clump of scrawny, dusty little trees it had somehow managed to assemble.

The first town across the Nebraska line was so different I declared a holiday, sat on a bench in the courthouse park and wrote a story. I rather think I've stumbled onto the best possible surroundings and state of mind in which to write. I certainly was more at home with it than at Harvard, home or Exeter.

That night I saw a rather interesting movie, "The Leathernecks." . . . It seems to me Richard Arlen is capable of pretty big stuff. I wish some one would give Von Sternberg a story for him. . . . Have to tackle a load now.

Jim

An extract from another letter, written in 1936, may be of interest:

It seems to me, comrades, that *New Masses* readers should treat Dostoevsky kindly yet strictly. There are inexcusable gaps and deviations in his ideology and they must not be condoned; on the other hand, we must not on their account make an enemy of a man who has come far and who may turn out to be inestimably useful to the Movement. (signed) Granville Hicks. I think *The Brothers Karamazov* deserves the co-operation of all the finest talents in Hollywood and wd. richly repay all research & expenditure. A fullsized replica, complete down to the last tpmizznmst, of the Mad Tsar Pierre (Charles Laughton). Papa Karamazov (Lionel Barrymore). His comic servant Grigory (Wallace Berry). Grigory's wife (Zasu Pitts). Smerdyakov (Charles Laughton). Smerdyakov's Familiar, a cat named Tabitha (Elsa Lanchester, the bride of Frankenstein). Zossima (Henry B. Walthall). . . . Miusov (Malcolm Cowley) . . . in Alyosha's Dream: Alyosha (Fred Astaire). Puck (Wallace Berry). Titania (Ginger Rogers or James Cagney). . . . Routines by Albertina Rasch. Artificial snow by Jean Cocteau. . . . Entire production supervised by Hugh Walpole. . . . To be played on the world's first Globular Screen, opening at the Hippodrome the night before *Jumbo* closes. Mr. Dostoevsky will be unable to appear at the opening but Charles A. Lindbergh has agreed to be on hand (you may recognize him by the smoked glasses & unassuming manner) and a troupe of selected ushers will throw epileptic fits during the intermission (courtesy Max Jacobs). Margaret Anglin will sell signed copies of Countee Cullen's *Medea* in the lobby. President Roosevelt will plant a tree. The Italian Expeditionary Force will observe two minutes silence in honor of the birth of the little Christ child. Artificial foreskins will be handed out at the north end of the

Wilhelmstrasse to anyone who is fool enough to call for them. The film will be preceded by *Glimpses of the New Russia,* photographed by M. Bourkeovitz [Margaret Bourke-White who, after her marriage to Erskine Caldwell, no foe of the Soviets, did do some such book of photographs, as I recall] . . . Suggested tie-ins for hinterland exhibitors: arrange to have your theatre picketted by your local chapters of the American Legion, the Catholic Church, the Parent-Teachers Association, the Sheetmetal Workers Union and the Youth for Peace Movement. Set up Jungle Shrubbery and a stuffed Gorilla in your lobby (your Police Station will be glad to furnish latter in return for a mention). If you are in the South, stage Negro Baptism (in white gowns) in front of your theatre. If in North, an Italian Saint's Day or a Jewish Funeral will do as well. Plug this feature hard. It will richly repay you.

Until I came to transcribe this, I had not realized how tasteless it is, calculated to offend the sensibilities of every right-thinking and wrong-thinking group in the country, minority or majority. It goes beyond buffoonery to express a nihilistic, destructive, irreverent, vulgar, alienated, un-American and generally lousy attitude. And why drag in the Sheetmetal Workers Union? And if the union, why the cops? There is something very old-fashioned about the whole thing, more like 1926 than 1936—and certainly not at all like 1962.

One of the unexpected things about Agee—and there were many, he was what used to be called "an original"—is that he was able to think in general terms without making a fool of himself, therein differing from most American creative writers of this century. This may have been because of his education or, more likely, because he had a gift that way. (He had so many gifts, including such odd ones, for intellectuals, as reverence and feeling.) Considering his hell-for-leather personality, Agee was a remarkably sophisticated, even circumspect, thinker. "Was just reading in *New Masses* Isidore Schneider welcoming Archie into the new pew," he wrote me in 1936.* "Still have my ways of believing in artforart and, more especially, of conviction. Marx—Marx plus Freud for that matter—isn't the answer to everything." Then he adds, with his typical balance, the last quality one would expect if one merely saw his picturesque side. "But just because Copernicus didn't settle all the problems of the universe is no reason at all to go on insisting that the sun moves around the earth and comes out a little southwest of purgatory." Jim was always moderate in an immoderate way, he was always out of step, and he had very little respect for the *Zeitgeist*. This was his tragedy and his triumph.

In his last letter to Father Flye, written a day or two before he died, Agee sketches out a fantasy about elephants—how they have been degraded by man from the most intelligent and the noblest of beasts to figures of fun. He felt he was dying and this was his last, most extraordinary insight. For wasn't this just what happened to him? Wasn't he also a large, powerful being who was put to base uses? The same note is struck in his fine parable, "A Mother's Tale"—also written toward the end of his life—in which a mother cow tells her children and nephews and nieces a strange tale that has come down through the generations about the ultimate fate of their kind. I venture that here too Agee was thinking of himself when he wrote about the slaughter of one species for the benefit of another. The cattle have their own life and purpose, as he did, and they are used by more powerful beings for a different purpose, as he was. This, at least, is how I imagine he may have thought, or rather felt (for it may not have been wholly conscious),

*The reference is to Archibald MacLeish, who had, under pressure from the *Zeitgeist*, temporarily edged over toward the Communists. Four years later the war had begun—no one ever had to ask Archie "Don't you know there's a war on?"—and MacLeish was attacking Dos Passos, Farrell, Hemingway and such as "The Irresponsibles" who had betrayed the American Dream. Shortly thereafter he was running Roosevelt's Office of Facts and Figures, as our wartime propaganda agency was at first quaintly called.

about it in his last years. It was emotionally true for him, and was also true in general. But looking at it more coldly, one must say something more. While Time, Inc., has in common with the Chicago packing houses one important thing—that its purpose is to convert something living, namely talent, into a salable commodity—it is not really an abattoir because those who, like Agee or myself, took its paychecks did so, unlike the cattle, of our own free will. The great question is, as Lenin once remarked of politics, who uses whom (I think he had a more pungent verb in the original Russian). It is possible to use instead of being used: Faulkner wrote Hollywood scripts for years. But Agee didn't have this kind of toughness and shrewdness. He was, in a way, too big and too variously talented.

There is something helpless about elephants precisely because of their combination of size and intelligence; it is a fact they can be tamed and trained as few wild animals can. It's not the fault of the tamers. Henry Luce was a decent fellow when Jim and I worked for him on *Fortune* and I'm sure Luce was, like me, charmed and impressed by Agee. But what a waste, what pathetic docility, what illusions! * As late

* On both sides. In *Fortune*'s case, they never really knew just where to have this strange creature. When he first arrived on *Fortune,* Agee speedily became, largely because nobody could figure out any other way to use him, the staff specialist in rich, beautiful prose on such topics as Rare Wines, Famous Orchid Collections, and The World's Ten Most Precious Jewels. When this finally reached the attention of Henry Luce, he was indignant, for he had a theory that a good writer could write on anything—also *Fortune* was supposed to be about business. He thought it somehow immoral that a writer should do only what he was best at—there was a lot of the Puritan in Luce. So he assigned to Agee as occupational therapy an article on The Price of Steel Rails, and furthermore announced he, Luce, would personally edit it (as he often did in those days). It was a fascinating topic for anyone with the slightest interest in economics, since the price of steel rails, which had been exactly the same for some fifty years, was the classic example of monopolistic price-fixing. But Agee, of course, had not even a slight interest in economics. He did his best and Luce did his best—"Now, Jim, don't you see . . . ?"—but finally Luce had to admit defeat and the article was assigned to someone else (me, I think) who did a workmanlike job. The trouble with Agee as a journalist was that he couldn't be just workmanlike, he had to give it everything he had, which was not good for him.

as 1945, after thirteen years with Time, Inc., Agee can still write to Father Flye that he has now been offered a job of "free-lance writing through all parts of the magazine," and this not in despair but hopefully. As if for a writer to be given the run of *Time* were not like a collector of sculpture being offered his pick of wax

figures from Madame Tussaud's Museum. He was always looking for a way out—in 1932, his first year on *Fortune*, he is wondering whether he shouldn't try for a Guggenheim grant; two years later he is asking Father Flye about the chances for a teaching job at Saint Andrew's, etc.—but he also was always full of innocent, elephantine hope.

In his perceptive introduction to the letters, Robert Phelps states that Jim got his job on *Fortune* because they were impressed by "an ingenious parody of *Time*" he had put out when he was editing the *Harvard Advocate.* I wish this were the whole story, but I remember in 1932 recommending Jim, then looking for a post-graduation job, to Ralph Ingersoll, then managing editor of *Fortune,* where I'd been working since my graduation from Yale. And I've dug up a letter from Jim which is almost unbearable in dramatic irony, the audience knowing how it is going to turn out: "Noted contents of your letter with eyes rolling upward and stomach downward with joy, relief, gratitude and such things. I shall send a wire in the morning to beat this letter down. . . . I don't want to miss any chances of losing this chance (for which thank you, God, and Managing Editor Ingersoll). . . . Words fail me re. the job: besides the fairly fundamental fact that I don't want to starve, there are dozens of other reasons I want *uh* job and many more why I am delighted to get this one."

But I didn't do him a favor, really.

2

James Agee's *A Death in the Family* is an odd book to be written by a serious writer in this country and century, for it is about death (not violence) and love (not sex). Death is conceived of in a most un-American way, not so much a catastrophe for the victim as a mystery, and at the same time an illumination, for the survivors. As for love, it is not sexual, not even romantic; it is domestic—between husband, wife, children, aunts, uncles, grandparents. This love is described tenderly, not in the tough, now-it-can-be-told style dominant in our fiction since Dreiser. The negative aspects are not passed over—Agee is, after all, a serious writer—but what he dwells on, what he "celebrates," is the positive affection that Tolstoy presented in "Family Happiness" but that now is usually dealt with in the women's magazines. Very odd.

There are other original features. We are used to novels that describe the professional and regional background more fully than the human beings, but here there is no "local color," and we are not even told what the father's occupation is. We are used to novels about "plain people" that are garnished with humanitarian rhetoric and a condescending little-man-what-now? pathos, as in *The Grapes of Wrath* and such exercises in liberal right-mindedness. But Agee felt himself so deeply and simply part of the world of his characters—the fact that they were his own family by no means explains this empathy—that he wrote about them as naturally as Mark Twain wrote about the people of Hannibal. The 1915 Tennessee vernacular sounds just right, not overdone yet pungent: " 'Well,' he said, taking out his watch. 'Good Lord a mercy!' He showed her. Three-forty-one. 'I didn't think it was hardly three. . . . Well, no more dawdling. . . . All right, Mary. I hate to go, but—can't be avoided.' " The last sentence, in rhythm and word choice, seems to me perfect. We are used, finally, to novels of action, novels of analysis, and novels that combine the two, but not to a work that is static, sometimes lyrical and sometimes meditative but always drawn from sensibility rather than from intellection. It reminds me most of Sherwood Anderson, another sport in twentieth-century American letters—brooding, tender-minded, and a craftsman of words.

James Agee died in 1955 at the age of forty-five. He died of a heart attack in a taxicab, and the platitudes about "shock" and "loss" suddenly became real. A friend I had for thirty years respected intellectually and sympathized with emotionally and disapproved of temperamentally and been stimulated by conversationally had vanished, abruptly and for good. I had always thought of Agee as the most broadly gifted writer of my generation, the one who, if anyone, might someday do major work. He didn't do it, or not much of it, but I am not the only one who expected he would. He really shouldn't have died, I kept thinking, and now this posthumous book makes me think it all the harder.

The book jacket is, for once, accurate when it describes Agee as "essentially a poet." For this is really not a novel but a long poem on themes from childhood and family life. The focal point is the death, in an automobile accident, of Jay Follet, a young husband and father who lived in Knoxville around the time of the First World War. This is about all that "happens." There are other episodes grouped around the death, and they are often vividly rendered, in novelistic terms, but there is no plot, no suspense, no development, and thus no novel. The point of view is mostly that of Jay's six-year-old son, Rufus, who is in fact James Agee, who is writing about his actual childhood and about the actual death of his father. Even those parts that are not told directly in terms of Rufus Agee's experience are affected by this viewpoint. The father and mother, although they are major figures, are barely individualized, since to a small child his parents are too close to be distinctly seen. The more distant and lesser figures, like Aunt Hannah, are more definite. Parents are big, vague archetypes to a child (Strength, Love, or—alas—Coldness, Failure), but aunts are people. In this child-centered structure, at least, *A Death in the Family* is in the American grain. (Why are our writers so much more at home with children than with adults?) Many of the best things are connected with Rufus: his delight over his new cap, his comic and appalling relations with his little sister, his nightmares ("and darkness, smiling, leaned ever more intimately inward upon him, laid open the huge, ragged mouth"), his innocent trust in the older boys, who tease and humiliate him with subtle cruelty. These parts of it can be recommended as an antidote to *Penrod*.

Agee was a very good writer. He had the poet's eye for detail. "Ahead, Asylum Avenue lay bleak beneath its lamps. . . . In a closed drug store stood Venus de Milo, her golden body laced in elastic straps. The stained glass of the L & N depot smoldered like an exhaused butterfly . . . an outcrop of limestone like a great bundle of dirty laundry. . . . Deep in the valley, an engine coughed and browsed." He could get magic into his writing the hardest way, by precise description:

> First an insane noise of violence in the nozzle, then the still irregular sound of adjustment, then the smoothing into steadiness and a pitch as accurately tuned to the size and style of stream as any violin . . . the short still arch of the separate big drops, silent as a held breath, and the only noise the flattering noise on leaves and the slapped grass at the fall of each big drop. That, and the intense hiss with the intense stream; that, and that same intensity not growing less but growing more quiet and delicate with the turn of the nozzle, up to that extreme tender whisper when the water was just a wide bell of film.

I haven't watered a lawn in forty years, but I remember that was the way it was in Sea Girt, New Jersey. And this was the way trolley cars were:

> A street car raising its iron moan; stopping, belling and starting; stertorous; rousing and raising again its iron increasing moan and swimming its gold windows and straw seats on past and past and past, the bleak spark crackling and cursing above it like a small malignant spirit set to dog its tracks; the iron whine rises on rising speed; still risen, faints; halts; the faint stinging bell; rises again, still fainter; fainting, lifting, lifts, faints forgone: forgotten.

These passages are from "Knoxville: Summer 1915," which appeared in *Partisan Review* twenty years ago; the publishers have had the good idea of reprinting it as a prelude to *A Death in the Family*. "We are now talking of summer evenings in Knoxville, Tennessee, in the time I lived there so successfully disguised to myself as a child," he begins, and he

concludes, "After a little I am taken in and put to bed. Sleep, soft smiling, draws me unto her: and those receive me, who quietly treat me, as one familiar and well-beloved in that home: but will not, oh, will not, not now, not ever; but will not ever tell me who I am." In between are five pages of reverie, lyrical and yet precise, about the after-dinner time when families sit around on porches and the fathers water the lawns. "Knoxville" is typical of Agee's prose: in the weighty authority with which words are selected and placed; in getting drama, as Dickens and Gogol did, out of description; in the cadenced, repetitive, sometimes Biblical rhythm; in the keyed-up emotion that teeters on the verge of sentimentality ("soft smiling" falls in, and "unto" comes too close for comfort); in the combination, usual only in writers of the first rank, of acute sensuousness with broad philosophical themes.

Although *A Death in the Family* is not a major

work, Agee, I think, had the technical, the intellectual, and the moral equipment to do major writing. By "moral," which has a terribly old-fashioned ring, I mean that Agee believed in and—what is rarer—was interested in good and evil. Lots of writers are fascinated by evil and write copiously about it, but they are bored by virtue; this not only limits their scope but prevents a satisfactory account of evil, which can no more be comprehended apart from good than light can be comprehended apart from darkness. Jay Follet is a good husband and father, Mary is a good wife and mother, and their goodness is expressed in concrete action, as is the evil in the boys who humiliate their son or the lack of "character" Jay's brother, Ralph, shows in a family crisis. (Character is another old-fashioned quality that interested Agee.) The theme is the confrontation of love, which I take to be life carried to its highest possible reach, and death, as the negation of life and yet a necessary part of it.

Admittedly, the book has its *longueurs,* and very long *longueurs* they are sometimes, but for the most part it is wonderfully alive. For besides his technical skill, his originality and integrity of vision, Agee had a humorous eye for human behavior. The nuances of the husband-and-wife relationship come out in a series of everyday actions: Mary peppering the eggs to Jay's taste; Jay straightening up the covers of the bed ("She'll be glad of that, he thought, very well pleased with the looks of it"); Mary insisting on getting up at three in the morning to cook breakfast for her husband, and his mixed reaction: "He liked night lunchrooms and had not been in one since Rufus was born. He was very faintly disappointed. But still more, he was warmed by the simplicity with which she got up for him, thoroughly awake." The bondage and the binding of marriage are both there. This is realism, but of a higher order than we have become accustomed to, since it includes those positive aspects of human relations which are so difficult to describe today without appearing sentimental. The uneasiness the Victorians felt in the presence of the base we feel in the presence of the noble. It is to Agee's credit that he didn't feel uneasy.

This livelier, more novelistic side of Agee appears in such episodes as the scene in which Aunt Hannah takes Rufus shopping for his first cap (up to then he had been allowed only babyish *hats*):

> He submitted so painfully conservative a choice, the first time, that she smelled the fear and hypocrisy behind it, and said carefully, "That is very nice, but suppose we look at some more, first." She saw the genteel dark serge, with the all but invisible visor, which she was sure would please Mary most, but she doubted whether she would speak of it; and once Rufus felt that she really meant not to interfere, his tastes surprised her. He tried still to be careful, more out of courtesy, she felt, then meeching, but it was clear to her that his heart was set on a thunderous fleecy check in jade green, canary yellow, black and white, which stuck out inches to either side above his ears and had a great scoop of a visor beneath which his face was all but lost. It was a cap, she reflected, which even a colored sport might think a little loud, and she was painfully tempted to interfere. Mary would have conniption fits. . . . But she was switched if she was going to boss him! "That's very nice," she said, as little drily as she could manage. "But think about it. Rufus. You'll be wearing it a long time, you know, with all sorts of clothes." But it was impossible for him to think about anything except the cap; he could even imagine how tough it was going to look after it had been kicked around a little. "You're very sure you like it," Aunt Hannah said.
>
> "Oh, yes," said Rufus.
>
> "Better than this one?" Hannah indicated the discreet serge.
>
> "Oh, yes," said Rufus, scarcely hearing her.
>
> "Or this one?" she said, holding up a sharp little checkerboard.
>
> "I think I like it best of all," Rufus said.
>
> "Very well, you shall have it," said Aunt Hannah, turning to the cool clerk.

Agee was a very American writer, and this passage, in its humor, its sensitivity to boyhood, its directness of approach, and its use of the rhythms and idioms of everyday speech, seems to me in the peculiarly American tradition of Twain and Anderson.

A Death in the Family should be read slowly. It is easy to become impatient, for the movement is circular, ruminative, unhurried. He dwells on things, runs on and on and on. Perhaps one *should* be impatient. What Agee needed was a sympathetically severe editor who would prune him as Maxwell Perkins pruned Thomas Wolfe, whom Agee resembled in temperament, though I think he was superior artistically. A better comparison is with Whitman, who also runs on and on, hypnotizing himself with his material, losing all sense of proportion, losing all sense of anyone else reading him, and simply chanting, in bardic simplicity, to himself. Like Whitman and unlike Wolfe, Agee was able at last to come down hard on The Point and roll it up into a magically intense formulation; the weariest river of Ageean prose winds somewhere safe to sea. After pages of excessive, obsessive chewing-over of a funeral, including a morbid detailing of the corpse's appearance and several prayers in full, Agee comes down, hard and accurate, to earth and to art: "[Rufus] looked towards his father's face and, seeing the blue-dented chin thrust upward, and the way the flesh was sunken behind the bones of the jaw, first recognized in its specific weight the word, *dead.* He looked quickly away, and solemn wonder tolled in him like the shuddering of a prodigious bell." Should one be impatient? I suspect one should. Granted the preceding *longueurs* were necessary for the writer if he were to work up enough steam for this climax, it doesn't follow that they are necessary for the reader. Would not a more conscious, self-disciplined writer have written them and then, when he had reached the final effect, have gone back and removed the scaffolding? It would have been interesting to see if Agee would have done this had he lived to give final form to *A Death in the Family.*

Agee was seldom able to tell when he was hitting it and when he wasn't. That he should have hit it so often is a sign of his talent. There are many passages in *A Death in the Family* that can only be called great, much though the word is abused these days, great in the union of major emotion with good writing.

In some literary circles, James Agee now excites the kind of emotion James Dean does in some nonliterary circles. There is already an Agee cult. This is partly because of the power of his writing and his lack of recognition—everyone likes to think he is on to a good thing the general public has not caught up with—but mainly because it is felt that Agee's life and personality, like Dean's, were at once a symbolic expression of our time and a tragic protest against it. It is felt that not their weakness but their vitality betrayed them. In their maimed careers and their wasteful deaths, the writer and the actor appeal to a resentment that intellectuals and teenagers alike feel about life in America, so smoothly prosperous, so deeply frustrating.

James Agee was born in Knoxville in 1909. He went to Saint Andrew's School there, then to Exeter and Harvard. In 1932, the year he graduated from Harvard, Agee got a job on *Fortune.* For fourteen years, like an elephant learning to deploy a parasol, Agee devoted his prodigious gifts to Lucean journalism. In 1939, he moved over to *Time,* where he wrote book reviews and then was put in charge of Cinema. In 1943, he began writing movie reviews for the *Nation,* too. He resigned from *Time* and the *Nation* in 1948, specifically to finish *A Death in the Family* but also because he realized that otherwise he would never get down to his own proper work. There was reason for his concern. Although he wrote constantly, in a small, shapely script that contrasted oddly with his oceanic personality, he finished very little; I remember grocery cartons full of manuscripts he had put aside. In 1948 he was thirty-nine, and he had published, aside from his journalism, only a book of poems, *Permit Me Voyage* (1934), and a long prose work, *Let Us Now Praise Famous Men* (1941).

In the seven years that were left to him, he did manage to bring *A Death in the Family* close to final form

and to publish a novelette, *The Morning Watch* (1951), and a short story, "A Mother's Tale" (*Harper's Bazaar*). But again most of his energies were diverted. For before he settled down to work in his old farmhouse in Hillsdale, New York, with his third wife, Mia, he had to get out of the way two profitable articles for *Life*, which he planned to knock out in six weeks and which took him six months. One was on silent-movie comedians; the second was on the films of John Huston. Agee had already, in 1947, written the commentary for one movie, *The Quiet One,* a documentary about Harlem life that was a great *succès d'estime,* but he had never worked in Hollywood. Huston liked his article, and commissioned him to do a script for a film version of Stephen Crane's *The Blue Hotel.* Huston never made the film, but he was impressed by Agee's script (and by Agee) and asked him to do one for *The African Queen.* This is mostly just another movie, but it does have several Agee touches —the Anglican service with only shining black faces in the congregation, Bogart's stomach rumblings at the tea party, the peculiar horror of the leeches and the gnats. It was ironical, and typical, that Agee's work with Huston was limited to a conventional adventure-romance film. Before they met, Huston made *The Red Badge of Courage,* and later he wanted Agee to work on *Moby Dick,* but Agee had an interfering commitment. So two jobs that would have given scope for his powers were lost by luck, or was it destiny? Whichever it was, it was rarely on his side.

After *The African Queen,* Agee did a number of other scripts—for *The Night of the Hunter,* which is realistic and at times macabre in a most un-Hollywoodian way; for a delightful short comedy, *The Bridge Comes to Yellow Sky,* taken from a story by Crane, in which he played the town drunk; for a film on the life of Gauguin (this, said to be his most remarkable script, was never used); for *Genghis Khan,* a Spanish-language Filipino film; for an "Omnibus" television series on the life of Lincoln; for a documentary about Williamsburg. Then he died.

Although he achieved much, it was a wasted, and wasteful, life. Even for a modern writer, he was extraordinarily self-destructive. He was always ready to sit up all night with anyone who happened to be around, or to go out at midnight looking for someone: talking passionately, brilliantly, but too much, drinking too much, smoking too much, reading aloud too much, making love too much, and in general cultivating the worst set of work habits in Greenwich Village. This is a large statement, but Agee's was a large personality. "I wish I knew how to work," he said to a friend. He wrote copiously, spending himself recklessly there, too, but there was too much else going on. He seemed to have almost no sense of self-preservation, allowing his versatility and creative energy to be exploited in a way that shrewder, cooler men of talent don't permit. His getting stuck for so long in the Luce organization is an instance; like Jacob, he drudged fourteen years in another man's fields, but there was no Rachel in view.

"Jim seemed to want to punish himself," another friend says. "He complicated his creative life so much that he was rarely able to come to simple fulfillment. He would put off work until he got far enough behind to feel satisfactorily burdened with guilt. Somehow he managed to turn even his virtues into weaknesses. Jim was bigger than life, had enormous energy—my God, the man was inexhaustible! He reacted excessively to *everything*. The trouble was he couldn't say No. He let people invade him, all kinds, anyone who wanted to. He thought he had time and energy enough for them all. But he didn't, quite. His heart trouble began on Huston's ranch out West, when he was working with him on the script of *The African Queen*. Huston was in the habit of playing two or three sets of singles before breakfast—*he* was a prodigal live-it-upper, too; that was one reason they got on so well together—and Agee, who hadn't played in years and was out of condition, went at it with him every morning, trying for every shot, until he collapsed on the court with his first heart attack. The doctors told Jim to take it easy, to drink, smoke, and live moderately. But that was the one talent he didn't have."

The waste one senses in Agee's career had other roots as well. He was spectacularly born in the wrong time and place. He was too versatile, for one thing. In art as in industry, this is an age of specialization. There is a definite if restricted "place" for poetry; there is even a Pulitzer Prize for it, and poets of far less capacity than Agee have made neat, firm little reputations. But his best poetry is written in prose and is buried in his three books. Nor was he solely dedicated to literature. Music was also important to him, and the cinema, so closely related to music, was his first love, and his last. I think he never gave up the dream of becoming a director, of expressing himself directly with images and rhythm instead of making do at one remove with words. His best writing has a cinematic flow and immediacy; his worst has a desperate, clotted quality, as though he felt that nobody would "get" him and was trying to break through, irritatedly, by brute exaggeration and repetition. But he was typed as a writer, and the nearest he could come to making movies was to write scripts—scripts that go far beyond what is usual in the way of precise indications as to sequence of shots, camera angles, visual details (the raindrops on a leaf are described in one), and other matters normally decided by the director. They are the scripts of a frustrated director.

The times might have done better by Agee. They could exploit one or two of his gifts, but they couldn't use him *in toto*—there was too much there to fit into any one compartment. In another sense, American culture was not structured *enough* for Agee's special needs; it was overspecialized as to function but amorphous as to values. He needed definition, limitation, discipline, but he found no firm tradition, no community of artists and intellectuals that would canalize his energies. One thinks of D. H. Lawrence, similar to Agee in his rebellious irrationalism, who was forced to define his own values and his own special kind of writing precisely because of the hard, clear, well-developed cultural tradition he reacted so strongly against.

If his native land offered Agee no tradition to corset his sprawling talents, no cultural community to moderate his eccentricities, it did provide "movements," political and aesthetic. Unfortunately, he couldn't sympathize with any of them. He was always unfashionable, not at all the thing for the post-Eliot thirties. His verse was rather conventional and romantic. In the foreword to *Permit Me Voyage,* Archibald MacLeish, than whom few have been more sensitive to literary fashions, accurately predicted, "It will not excite the new-generationers, left wing or right. . . . Agee does not assume . . . a Position." Ideologically, it was even worse. In an age that was enthusiastic about social issues, Agee's whole style of being was individualistic and antiscientific. He was quite aware of this; oddly, considering the constellation of his traits, he had a strong bent toward ideas. Unlike, say, Thomas Wolfe, he was an intellectual; it was another aspect of his versatility. This awareness comes out clearly in a passage from that extraordinary grab bag *Let Us Now Praise Famous Men:*

> "Description" is a word to suspect.
>
> Words cannot embody; they can only describe. But a certain kind of artist, whom we will distinguish from others as a poet rather than a prose writer, despises this fact about words or his medium, and continually brings words as near as he can to an illusion of embodiment. [Here the frustrated moviemaker speaks, for if words cannot embody, pictures can, and without illusion—a picture is an artistic fact in itself, unlike a word.] In doing so he accepts a falsehood but makes, of a sort in any case, better art. It seems very possibly true that art's superiority over science and over all other forms of human activity, and its inferiority to them, reside in the identical fact that art accepts the most dangerous and impossible of bargains and makes the best of it, becoming, as a result, both nearer the truth and farther from it than those things which, like science and scientific art, merely describe, and those things which, like human

beings and their creations and the entire state of nature, merely are, the truth.

As MacLeish observed, Agee appealed neither to the Left nor to the Right. "I am a Communist by sympathy and conviction," he wrote in the thirties, and at once went on to put a tactless finger right on the sore point:

> But it does not appear (just for one thing) that Communists have recognized or in any case made anything serious of the sure fact that the persistence of what once was insufficiently described as Pride, a mortal sin, can quite as coldly and inevitably damage and wreck the human race as the most total power of "Greed" ever could: and that socially anyhow, the most dangerous form of pride is neither arrogance nor humility, but its mild, common denominator form, complacency. . . . Artists, for instance, should be capable of figuring the situation out to the degree that they would refuse the social eminence and the high pay they are given in Soviet Russia. The setting up of an aristocracy of superior workers is no good sign, either.

The idiom ("the sure fact . . . figuring the situation out . . . no good sign, either") and the rhythm are in the American vernacular, and thus hopelessly out of key with the style in which everybody else wrote about these matters then. Nor was Agee any more congruous with the Right. Although he was deeply religious, he had his own kind of religion, one that included irreverence, blasphemy, obscenity, and even communism (of his own kind). By the late forties, a religio-conservative revival was underway, but Agee felt as out of place as ever. "If my shapeless comments can be of any interest or use," he characteristically began his contribution to a *Partisan Review* symposium on Religion and the Intellectuals, "it will be because the amateur and the amphibian should be represented in such a discussion. By amphibian I mean that I have a religious background and am 'pro-religious'—though not on the whole delighted by this so-called revival—but doubt that I will return to religion." Amateurs don't flourish in an age of specialization, or amphibians in a time when educated armies clash by night.

The incompatibility of Agee and his times came to a head in the sensational failure of Agee's masterpiece, *Let Us Now Praise Famous Men.* It is a miscellaneous book, as hard to classify as that earlier failure *Moby Dick,* which it resembles, being written in a "big" style, drawing poetry from journalistic description, and making the largest statements about the human condition. It is mostly a documentary account of three southern tenant-farming families, illustrated with thirty-one magisterial photographs by Walker Evans, Agee's close friend, who is listed on the title page as co-author and whose influence was strong on the text. But it is many other things as well—philosophy, narrative, satire, cultural history, and autobiography. It is a young man's book—exuberant, angry, tender, willful to the point of perversity, with the most amazing variations in quality; most of it is extremely good, some of it is as great prose as we have had since Hawthorne, and some of it is turgid, mawkish, overwritten. But the author gives himself wholly to his theme and brings to bear all his powers; he will go to any lengths to get it just right. From this emerges a truth that includes and goes beyond the truth about poverty and ignorance in sociological studies (and "realistic" novels), the truth that such squalid lives, imaginatively observed, are also touched with the poetry, the comedy, the drama of what is unexpected and unpredictable because it is living. It is illuminating to compare Agee's book with one of those New Deal surveys of "the sharecropping problem." It is also interesting to read a professional work on grade-school education and then to read Agee's twenty-seven pages of notes on the subject:

> Adults writing to or teaching children: in nearly every word within these textbooks, for instance [he has three devastating pages on one of them, which every writer for children should read], there is a flagrant mistake of

some kind. The commonest is this: that they simplify their own ear, without nearly enough skepticism as to the accuracy of the simplification, and with virtually no intuition for the child or children; then write or teach to satisfy that ear; discredit the child who is not satisfied, and value the child who, by docile or innocent distortions of his intelligence, is.

The "esthetic" is made hateful and is hated beyond all other kinds of "knowledge." It is false-beauty to begin with; it is taught by sick women or sicker men; it becomes identified with the worst kinds of femininity and effeminacy; it is made incomprehensible and suffocating to anyone of much natural honesty and vitality.

The book grew out of an assignment to Agee and Evans from *Fortune* in 1936 to do a story on southern sharecroppers. For two months they lived in the Alabama back country. *Fortune,* unsurprisingly, couldn't "use" the article. Harper then staked Agee to a year off the Luce payroll to write the book. When it was done, they couldn't use it either; they wanted deletions in the interests of good taste, and Agee refused; since the higher-ups weren't enthusiastic anyway about this strange, difficult work, Harper stood firm. Finally, Houghton Mifflin bought it out in 1941. The critics disliked it—Selden Rodman, Lionel Trilling, and George Marion O'Donnell were honorable exceptions—and it sold less than six hundred copies the first year. *Moby Dick* sold five hundred, which was six times as good a showing, taking into account the increase of population.

The mischance that dogged Agee's career is evident in the timing of his death. Those who knew him best say that in the last few years of his life Agee changed greatly, became more mature, more aware of himself and of others, shrewder about his particular talents and problems. In the very last year, he had even begun to pay some attention to doctors' orders. He was by then getting such good fees for scripts that he was looking forward to doing only one a year and spending the rest of the time on his own writing. He might even have found out who he was. *A Death in the Fam-*

ily contrasts significantly with *Let Us Now Praise Famous Men.* It rarely achieves the heights of the earlier book—I think Agee's literary reputation will be mostly based on about half of *Let Us Now Praise Famous Men*—but it is written in a more controlled and uniform style; it has more humor and none of the self-consciousness that often embarrasses one in the earlier work; its structure is classical, without Gothic excrescences; and, most significant of all, human beings are seen objectively, with the novelist's rather than the poet's eye. There is also the remarkable short story, "A Mother's Tale," he wrote three years before his death: a Kafka-like allegory, perfectly ordered and harmonious all through, of the human situation in this age of total war. I think only a thoroughly developed writer could have done it. Like Keats, Agee died just when he was beginning to mature as an artist. That Keats was twenty-five and Agee forty-five doesn't alter the point. Agee was an American, of a race that matures slowly, if ever.

"He was at his best just short of his excesses, and he tended in general to work out toward the dangerous edge. He was capable of realism . . . but essentially he was a poet. . . . He had an exorbitant appetite for violence, for cruelty, and for the Siamese twin of cruelty, a kind of obsessive tenderness which at its worst was all but nauseating. . . . In his no longer fashionable way, he remained capable, and inspired. He was merely unadaptable and unemployable, like an old, sore, ardent individualist among contemporary progressives. . . . He didn't have it in him to be amenable, even if he tried." So Agee wrote after D. W. Griffith died. He may have been describing the film director. He was certainly describing himself.

"I See Him . . ."

John Huston

IT'S ALL to the good that so many of you now know James Agee's writing—his novels, his criticism, his poetry. (In a sense it was all poetry.) I wish that you could also have known Jim himself.

Let me begin by describing him physically. He was about six-two and heavy but neither muscular nor fat—a mountaineer's body. His hair was dark brown, his eyes blue and his skin pale. His hands were big and slab-like in their thickness. He was very strong, and except for one occasion, which I only heard about, when he stove a *Time* editor against the wall, he was always gentle toward his fellow humans with that kind of gentleness usually reserved for plants and animals.

His clothes were dark and shiny. I can't imagine him in a new suit. Black shoes scuffed grey, wrinkled collar, a button off his shirt and a raveled tie—he wore clothes to be warm and decent. Jim's elegance was inward. I doubt whether he had any idea of what he looked like, or whether he ever looked in a mirror except to shave. Vanity wasn't in him.

He held his body in very slight regard altogether, feeding it with whatever was at hand, allowing it to go to sleep when there was nothing else for it to do, begrudging it anything beneficial such as medicine when he was sick. On the other hand, he was a chain smoker and a bottle-a-night man.

You who didn't actually know Jim might wish that he had taken better care of himself and lived longer to write more novels and screenplays . . . more poetry. But we who did know him recognize the fact that his body's destruction was implicit in his makeup, and we thank heaven that it was strong enough to withstand for so many years the constant assaults he leveled on it.

I was with Jim at the time of his first heart attack, and while he did obey the doctors' orders over a period of weeks—out of respect for their profession—and never asked any of his friends to get him a drink or even give him a drag off a cigarette, he let it be clearly understood that once the crisis was past he intended to resume the habits of life that had led up to it. I can hear myself uttering some nonsense about doing things in moderation, like sleeping eight hours every night and smoking say half a pack of cigarettes a day and only having a drink or two before dinner. Jim nodded his head in mute agreement with everything I said, or if not agreement, sympathy. And he went on nodding until I faltered and finished. Then he smiled his gentle smile and, after a decent interval, changed the subject.

His regard for other people's feelings was unique in my experience. I don't believe it was because he was afraid of hurting them, and certainly it had nothing to do with gaining in anyone's estimation. It was simply that his soul rejoiced when he could say yes and mean it to something someone else believed in.

He never attempted to win anyone to his way of thinking, far less to try to prove anyone mistaken or in the wrong. He would take a contrary opinion—regardless of how foolish it was—and hold it up to the light and turn it this way and that, examining its facets as though it were a gem of great worth, and if it turned out to be a piece of cracked glass, why then he, Jim, must have misunderstood—the other fellow had meant something else, hadn't he . . . *this,* perhaps? And sure enough Jim would come up with some variation of the opinion that would make it flawless as a specimen jewel. And the other fellow would be

very proud of having meant precisely that, and they would go on from there.

I can see him sitting on the edge of a chair, bunched forward, elbows on knees, arms upraised, the fingers of one of the slab-like hands pointing at those of the other and working as if they were trying to untie a knot. His forehead is furrowed and his mouth is twisted in concentration. His head is nodding in sympathy and understanding. He is smiling. Gaps show between his teeth. (Jim only went to the dentist to have a tooth pulled, never fixed.)

He is smiling. It stops raining all over the world. A great discovery has been made. He and another are in complete agreement. We who beheld that smile will never forget it.

Jim's Many Gestures

Florence Homolka

JIM HAD a deep sympathy for the poor of this world—for those who were materially poor in terms of this world's goods, certainly, but most especially for those who were at a loss in life, whose minds were inadequate, whose feelings were of little account to anyone. In movies, which he liked so much and took so seriously, he would often point out nameless members of the cast with appreciation.

He always used his hands a great deal in talking. He searched so carefully, and at the same time so violently and at such length, for the exact way to express himself that it amounted almost to inarticulacy. He had great persistence: he would never give up trying to explain something he had set out to clarify, and his struggle for communication often took the form of reading out loud from his own works, or those of others. He studied hard and long and sincerely, and it is sad that his end came just as he was finding ways of telling what he had to tell, not only through the printed page, but also through film, which had become such a close part of his vision and consciousness. He was awarded the Pulitzer Prize more than a year after he died in a taxi that was taking him to his doctor for a heart examination. In his ironical way, he would have enjoyed this circumstance. He would have made a long embroidered anecdote out of it, telling it with his slight lisp, and many gestures.

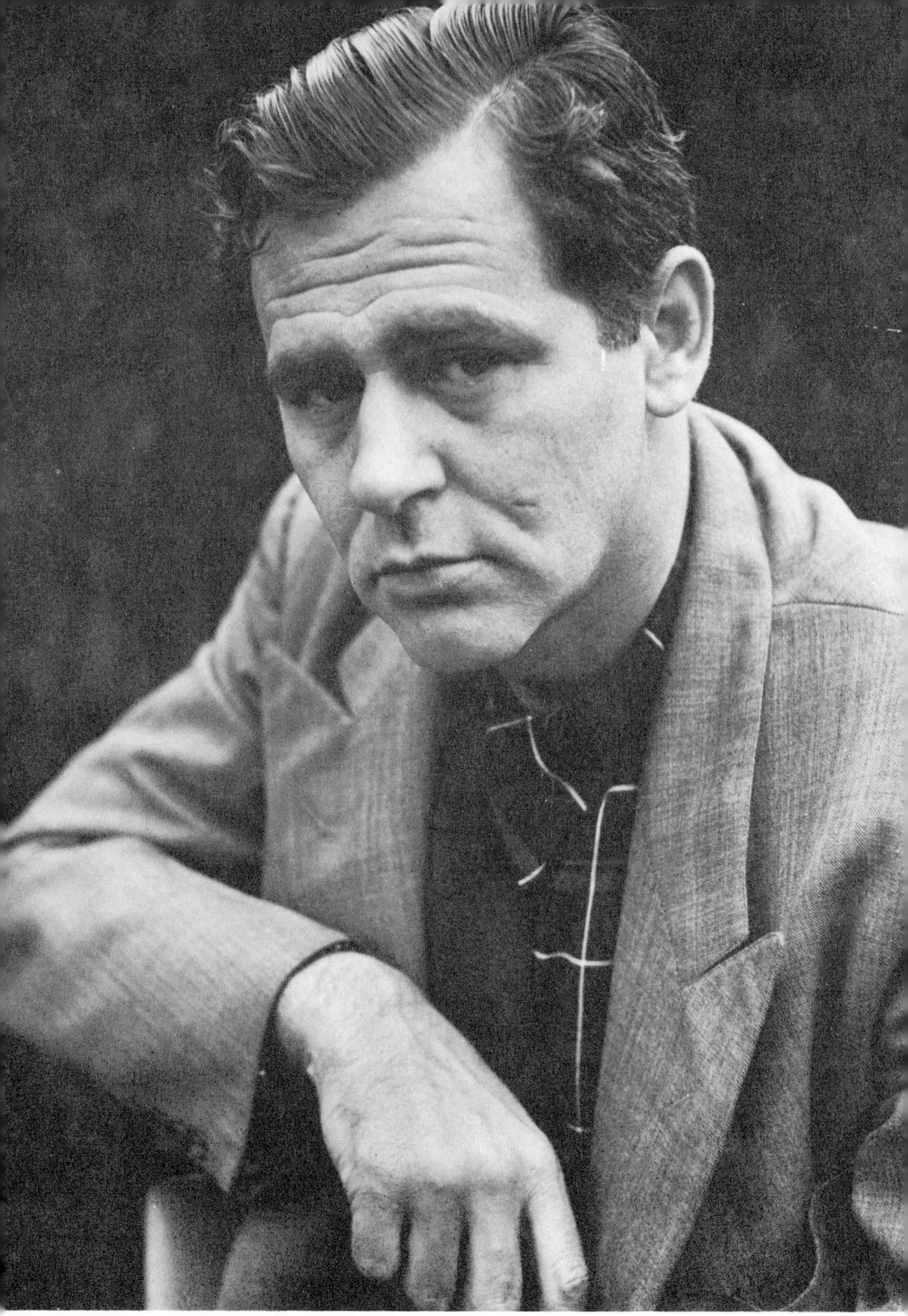

Agee

Whittaker Chambers

THERE IS ALWAYS a certain presumption in publicly claiming close friendship with someone whom we have long felt to be greater than ourselves, especially when the world, or a part of it, has belatedly discovered that there was greatness in him, and when he is no longer here to say of us: Yes, that is how it was; or: No, I felt about it a little differently. I am speaking about James Agee, who died in 1955 of a heart attack. I want you to know that I recognize the presumption and I shall risk it anyway. . . . What I shall say is my tribute to my friend, whose grave on his quiet farm I have not seen, and may not get to see, but approach in this way.

In fact, life had separated us for several years before. I was engaged in certain well-known events. Later, I was confined about two years, writing a book. Jim was in Hollywood, working with John Huston. Then came two heart attacks in quick succession. From his sick room came, too, seven- and eight-page letters, penciled in the minute, slantwise, beautiful script which was a personal cipher that took hours to decode. In the spring of 1952, we both happened into New York. Jim came unexpectedly to my hotel, and we walked down Fifth Avenue together—very slowly, he could only inch along now, so that I saw that he was taking his last walks. He stopped before a show window in which cruelly elegant mannequins in exaggerated posture swam in a sickly lavender light. He stared at them for awhile. Then, "It's a pansy's world," he said, looking at them and at the city around us. We laughed. It was a summing up. Later, I bought two chocolate Easter eggs for his little girls. And that is how we parted. It is my last vivid memory of the living man. A few months later, I was in a hospital with a heart of my own. At Christmas, Jim sent me a dwarfed pear tree which somebody planted for me. When I could get about, I helped it to live under some adverse conditions. Those days all run together in weakness to form a blur. In that blur Jim died, and his death became part of the blur.

Multas per gentes et multa per aequora vectus,
Venio, frater, ad has inferias.

Carried through many people and over many waters,
I come, my brother, to these [sad] rites of death.
—Catullus

For me the blur passed into an upland spell and then again into blur. In the autumn of 1955 I was unloading a truck load of hay bales—the last load of the year's last cutting of alfalfa. It was a foolish thing to do. But the day is what the day is: we do what needs doing. Before half the load was off, a heart attack.

Then the long weeks in bed while the cold came, the earth hardened, it was winter, and at last a new year. During those long silent days I read a good first novel, *Your Own Beloved Sons* by Thomas Anderson. It was about the Korean War. There was the usual misery of the front line in winter—a hardened landscape of snow not too different from that outside my window. There were familiar types, too. There was the sensitive, callow, bookish soldier named Littlejohn, and, by a stroke, nicknamed Little John. There was the crude non-com. Little John was cooking and the non-com grabbed his book. Little John tried to get it back. The book was James Agee's *The Morning Watch.* The non-com tormented Little John by suggesting that it was sex stuff. Little John felt this as a violation. He tried to explain. It did not make sense. But then he said it: "It's about religion, but it's not a religious book." Yes, that was it, that was absolutely it.

I laid the book on the bed. It seemed to me that, for the first time in years, Jim came walking toward me across a frozen field. I could see him as we can so seldom wholly visualize the dead. And, as we met, the little nod of the head, casual but so oddly reserved, and the hands clutched against the stomach in a gesture of pain, and on the face a grimace of pain—a mocking grimace. Anybody who knew Jim well knew that gesture and that grimace.

A heart attack sets the mind to living naturally with the possibility of a sudden end. As the swift and unexpected image passed, I smiled. Its place was taken by another, humorous and rather solemn one. It was an image of myself at the Judgment, with God the Father bending a little to press a little grimly, and asking me: "Will anyone speak for this man?" Then from the seraphic side lines Jim would step out—unshaved as nearly always, work shirt, workmen's shoes, corduroy trousers, as usual—and stand in silence beside me. And God the Father would half smile with the little gesture of the hand that means: "What can you do?" As we step back into the crowd, from the vault and from the depths, the choirs would sing in those pure tones. In all that throng, Jim, I thought, would be the only one who did not know that they were singing about him.

A sick man's thoughts about a dead man? Yes. Of course. Jim drank too much—in the end he largely drank himself to death. He was savagely unconventional, and, in most practical matters of life, belligerently irresponsible. Certain things—rudeness, in particular—moved him to violence. He once drove his fist through the door of a Fifth Avenue bus, which its driver had insolently refused to open for him. He was not a religious man, not in most senses understood by the Westminster Confession, which was Jim's. But he was, among all men I have known—telling them over carefully in my mind—the one who was most "about religion."

Faint Lines in a Drawing of Jim

Mia Agee,
with Gerald Locklin

THE DIFFICULTY in composing a memoir such as this is that I know it can't be done. There is no possible way for me to evaluate or select specific telling instances that reveal anything of significance in relation to as complex a personality as James Agee's. The person closely involved in randomly selecting and relating such happenings must surely know how fragile such an eclectic process is. My memories have been carefully walled off and I know what a dangerous endeavor it is to suddenly open such doors. I am also unable to relate everyday events in a modulated tone of voice, and with the kind of distance that the passage of time is supposed to provide. So why am I in these pages at all? I agree that I probably shouldn't be, but I also felt like joining a personal memorial without really facing in any detail the realities that this would involve for me.

There has been much written about James Agee and his work since his death and I have nothing but appreciation for most of it. I am, however, struck by how often his critics talk about his having "wasted his time and diffused his talent." The justification given normally cites the many years he worked for magazines such as *Fortune, Time,* and the *Nation,* magazines by whom he was employed. To these are added all the many months he worked in Hollywood doing scripts for movies that saw production or a few that didn't. In addition there are those innumerable commentaries that had to be written for foreign films —mostly documentaries. It is true that he had to work very hard at all these jobs and whatever writing he could do of his own had to be squeezed into off hours, and there were never enough of them. However, the question still remains whether in fact this was a waste of time. I am not convinced of it. It is true he may have stayed with some of these jobs too long, but would it really have been any less wasteful had he spent his days in an advertising agency, or driving a New York cab, or becoming a dirt farmer in the Tennessee mountains? What do writers do when they have to make a living? Is it really assumed today that a writer writes because he has a private income; or is it assumed that he teaches at a college and that teaching is less a waste of time or perhaps less time-consuming, or is it simply more intellectually acceptable? Personally I see very little difference in writing for a magazine which at least uses some of the skills a writer is most interested in having. I know that Jim to some extent felt challenged by the idea of having to write within a set format but working at all times against that format, creating a kind of tension and seeing just how far he could go. I know for a fact that he enjoyed having to write long mechanical process captions as he did for *Fortune,* such as how a certain fabric was loomed or how glass was formed or how arbitrage works. These tasks had some of the intriguing characteristics of certain games and puzzles, and in Jim's hands they became small poems. Henry R. Luce wanted to send him to the Harvard Business School because he wanted to see that kind of writing applied to a corporation story (then *Fortune*'s major journalistic invention). Luce couldn't really see why Jim declined this offer. I must say I would have been interested to see such a corporation story, though I doubt that *Fortune* would ever have printed it.

Jim tried, of course, other ways of making money. *Let Us Now Praise Famous Men* was worked on for more than two years after he left *Fortune,* without any personal reserves and an advance from the publisher of something around $500—an advance the book in fact never made back. Of course he had to have a regular job again and he went back to *Time* to write book reviews. Since he was a slow reader and never wanted to be a speedy one he moved into movies, and as a movie reviewer he opened up a new field for himself, though a field with which he had always been in love. He stayed on as a film critic for roughly eight years and every few years he would try to break out of the bind by trying for grants, awards, etc., but he never made it. He finally did get out by committing himself to do some free-lance articles for *Life* only to discover that despite the fact that the articles were well paid, they consumed infinitely more time than his regular jobs did and so in effect paid him less.

Add to this the fact that Jim was a married man for most of his adult life and that for a large part of it he had children to support, and it seems suprising how much of his own work he did get done. He was a very hard and constant worker. He was at all times at work on one or more projects of his own and was always dissatisfied with himself for not getting more of his own work done. So the waste of talent is perhaps not so much a real waste, *i.e.,* not having done enough writing, but a discrepancy between the talent and the tasks to which it was put. That too I think is largely debatable. One could argue that Jim's employment after all resulted in some very fine writing. His film criticisms are considered classics—his serious treatment of what were then called movies and now called films was far ahead of its time. *Let Us Now Praise Famous Men,* though eventually rejected by *Fortune,* did germinate from a journalistic assignment. His screenplays are a part of every film enthusiast's library, and many of his most powerful attitudes derived from his journalistic exposure to the ideas and realities of his time.

Jim worked better in some places than in others and better under some conditions than others. The best environment for him to work in was, without doubt, in the country. This was particularly true of our place in Hillsdale. The old farmhouse is about six miles from the nearest town; it lies on the outskirts of the Berkshire mountains, and the house sits on top of a hill with woods all around it and no other place in sight. There was no electricity and only an old gravity water system which broke down most of the time so that the water had to be pumped or carried. But the place has an indescribable stillness, tranquillity, and peacefulness. This is where Jim could work best. This is where he wrote his first film script *The Blue Hotel*, a Stephen Crane story; he did it in four days, and it was a kind of tour de force. This was the place where he could recharge his psychic batteries and where he would arise early and start his work about six or seven in the morning. He would get to sleep when it got dark and he would feel in tune and happy. He would often go there by himself when he had a lot of work to do, and the children and I would stay in the city busy with our own things. On weekends and vacations we would all of us go there and everyone of us developed a particular affection for the place.

Jim had many friends in the city and he valued his friendships highly, but he was not in love with the city itself and it was basically a hard place for him to do his own writing. He loved many of the stimulations and possibilities New York offered, and because he was by nature a gregarious person, much of the stimulation involved people and parties and music. He never needed much outside pressure to turn into a night person and would often try to work after the party was over and know that probably all he was good for by that time was writing some letters he needed to write and which he knew he didn't have to mail the next day if he didn't like them. Serious work during the night he could do only if he had worked straight through. He was extremely musical and played the piano well and with a powerful style of his own. Aside from a large classical repertoire which included everything from chamber music to opera, he also loved jazz and blues. He had a great collection of old jazz records, Bess Smith, Louis Armstrong, etc., but he always felt that his jazz improvisations on the piano were not very good. He had a real affection for old church hymns and felt that it would be fun to write a history of the United States in terms of the popularity of church hymns and the faiths they represented. It was one of the things I could not share with him since, aside from the fact that I knew very little about them, I didn't like what I did know of them. He was extremely careful with his selection of hymns for some of the movie scripts he worked on, and both *The African Queen* and *The Night of the Hunter* made dramatic use of his selections.

Jim had the ability to give himself totally to whatever he was doing at the moment, much as a child does. It made little difference whether this was writing, playing tennis or piano, or talking to someone. He was a good listener but he was a better talker. He could get involved in a meaningful conversation with absolutely anyone and people tended to be dazzled by it. This did not always work in his favor. There is the story of his going to meet a publisher who was interested in one of his manuscripts (I think it was *The Morning Watch*); after spending a couple of hours with him, Jim left and the publisher turned down the manuscript without reading it because he was totally convinced that a man who could talk that way obviously couldn't write. I guess it must be unusual to be able to excel at talking and writing both.

In some ways he was an old-fashioned man. He was a man who took pride in *all* his writing; he never tossed off anything in his life and he was incapable of a hack job. To honor verbal agreements was more important to him than legal ones. For example, he made a verbal agreement with a Filipino actor, Emmanuel Conde, to direct a film for and with him in the Philippines. While Jim was waiting in New York for

Conde to contact him and finishing some previous work commitments, John Huston came to town ready to get started on their long-planned project of *Moby Dick,* a book both Huston and Jim had talked of doing together for years, and a story they both had very special feelings for. This also involved an invitation to go to Europe (Ireland and Southern France) for a year, a prospect which made me drool and which Jim would have loved to do. To my utter dismay, Jim, who was excited about both the trip and the script, told Huston that he couldn't do it at this time because of his previous agreement with Conde. Huston thought the decision insane and proceeded to get another scriptwriter. Nobody knows what happened to Mr. Conde or his project since nobody ever heard from him again. Huston did direct *Moby Dick* with Ray Bradbury as his writer, but Jim never saw the film.

I'm sometimes asked in what direction I think Jim would have gone in his career if he had had another five, ten, or twenty years to live. Of course he wanted to direct films and I am sure he would have done so. As early as his Harvard years he set forth one summer on a quixotic trip to Hollywood, an abortive hitchhiking trip which ended in the Middle West harvesting. Had he arrived there, I am not at all sure he would ever have returned to Harvard. He had a passion for movies. Today this is true of many young people but in Jim's generation it was unusual for a young man with his education and talent to consider movies as a significant new art form and not simply as entertainment.

To speculate about what he might have done as a writer had he lived seems futile, since so little is left of notebooks and manuscripts. Most of his papers were stolen while in storage in his sister's house. He had done some preliminary work on a novel about modern marriage. He wanted very much to get back to poetry, and he was planning an original film script. That is all I know.

Jim had a great sense of humor and always wanted to do more humorous writing. He could be a wicked satirist, and some of his oldest friendships were largely involved with a shared style of humor and satire—Wilder Hobson for example and Dwight Macdonald. When meeting at parties they would set each other off into imitations, parodies, and puns, and outdo each other in spontaneous inventions.

The role of father both attracted and terrified him. Not really a contradiction but simply a characteristic double feeling about important matters, taken very seriously. He had an appreciation of babies, probably relating to their mute expressiveness and their wide open potential. It seems that other poets such as Byron shared this fascination. When I was working for *Fortune* and wanted to go to Europe for a three-month assignment, I planned to make special provisions for the care of the children, but he insisted that he wanted to take care of them himself. My misgivings were misplaced, and they all enjoyed being on their own.

He was a magnificent, warm, sensitive, contradictory, passionate, compassionate human being, but he was psychologically incapable of moderation, even during the period of his last illness. His motto was "a little bit too much is just enough for me." I am asked was he self-destructive? Obviously in a sense he was, and since he was a romantic, he was strongly disinclined to let himself be programed by necessities and external realities. He was always full of good intentions for reform and discipline in the wake of a severe setback, but his reforms never lasted very long. He had a very strong physique and so was always able to count on his body doing what he wanted it to.

Possibly, as part of his religious upbringing, as well as a strong poetic sensibility, he had an alive religious nerve of some kind and he conceived life as basically tragic. His tendency toward self-pity was more a pity for humanity which happened to include himself. He had a strongly developed sense of guilt, a sense of guilt that at times could paralyze him and that at the same time formed a very basic part of his character. He said that I had pointed out to him that his greatest weakness was self-pity, where he had always felt that it was a weakness of will. I am not so sure that they are not essentially the same.

He was never ill until his first heart attack in 1951. As a result he was constitutionally an unlikely candidate for the role of invalid or even the role of a man who has to budget his physical strength, has to be careful about what he eats, drinks, smokes, etc. All his instincts worked along an absolute assumption of physical well-being and the ability to be careless about physical strength. He loved to play tennis, hadn't played it in New York for many years, and was delighted to start playing again when he came to California. He ignored the fact that he was out of training, that his life had been largely sedentary, and that he was no longer twenty-five years old. He started playing singles at seven o'clock in the morning, after having worked all night writing, with an enthusiasm that was best and most accurately described as a bull charging on red cloth. This produced his first heart attack and that was the reason he wasn't able to go to Africa for the filming of *The African Queen,* a trip he had been very much looking forward to.

I have been asked to what extent I think of Jim as being southern. Naturally I don't think of him as the stereotype Southern Gentleman but yes, I do think of him as being southern. A certain kind of sensitivity and gentleness and true courteousness to me are part of this. I think I associate those qualities most perhaps with his father's Tennessee mountain background. I myself have a feeling for the South that has nothing to do with any contemporary clichés, and to this day, I find that people in the South establish a more immediate, more simple human contact with me. Traveling through the South, I can stop for coffee at a little roadside place and come away a half an

hour later feeling that I have been in some simple communication, recognized as another human being rather than a traveling android.

Jim had an enormous empathy with people. No doubt this was due in part to his imagination, but it was also a function of his essential humanness. He saw other people's dilemmas and seemed always able to respond. This of course was time consuming. He was a generous man, both with money and time. He had, during his life, fluctuated between having no money, having little money, and having occasionally a fair amount of money. He never became accustomed to those various levels. Even when he had money, setting out on a trip, he would pull into a gasoline station and ask for a dollar's worth of gas (a Depression habit). Contrarily, at a critical time he would buy me three evening gowns to cheer me up, though I never used evening gowns; but they were very pretty. He hated to have to think about money and he didn't do much of it except in extremities. One day I got a call from the cleaner to whom Jim had taken his suit to be pressed and he told me he found $450 in Jim's pants pocket. He had just cashed a paycheck, changed his suit, and never missed it.

I have tried to follow a sequence of questions about Jim which have been put to me and I hope I have at least partially answered them, but what does it all add up to? Maybe the best thing would be not to try to add anything up, but simply let it go as faint lines in a drawing that may eventually form a pattern but that so far is indistinguishable as a portrait.

Chronology of Events

1909 **November 27**
James Rufus Agee born in Knoxville, Tennessee.

1916 **May 18**
Agee's father, Hugh James Agee, killed in auto accident.

1919 **Autumn**
Enters Saint Andrew's, a boarding school for boys; meets Father Flye and his wife, who lived on school grounds.

1924
Agee's mother marries Father Erskine Wright, bursar at Saint Andrew's; they move to Rockland, Maine.

1925 **Summer**
Visits France and England with Father Flye.

Autumn
Enters Phillips Exeter Academy, Exeter, New Hampshire.
Corresponds with Dwight Macdonald.

1927
Elected editor of Exeter *Monthly* and president of Lantern Club (literary club).

1928 **Autumn**
Enters Harvard University; Robert Saudek is his roommate.

1929 **Summer**
Works in Nebraska and Kansas.

1930
Robert Fitzgerald is his classmate in Robert Hillyer's and I. A. Richards' classes.

1931
Agee is president of *Harvard Advocate.*

May
"The Truce," a short story, published in *Harvard Advocate.*

1932 Spring
Graduates from Harvard, and as a result of a parody issue of *Time* and of Dwight Macdonald's efforts, is engaged as a cub reporter, then as a regular staff writer for *Fortune* in Chrysler Building.

1933 January 28
Marries Olivia Saunders.

1934 October
Permit Me Voyage published in Yale Series of Younger Poets, with foreword by Archibald MacLeish.

1935 November to May, 1936
Leave of absence from *Fortune;* lives and writes in Anna Maria, Florida.

1936 Spring
Attends David McDowell's commencement at Saint Andrew's while visiting Father Flye.

Summer
Spends eight weeks with Walker Evans in Alabama, interviewing and photographing tenant families for a series of *Fortune* articles.

1938 Spring
Moves to 27 Second Street, Frenchtown, New Jersey.
Marries Alma Mailman.

1939 Summer
Delivers manuscript of *Three Tenant Families* to Harper's.
Begins reviewing books for *Time* with Whittaker Chambers.
Robert Fitzgerald works with Agee at *Time.*
T. S. Matthews is Agee's editor at *Time.*

1939

Moves to Saint James Place, Brooklyn, New York.

1940 March 20
First son, Joel, born.
Agee moves to West 15th Street.
Robert Fitzgerald leaves *Time.*

1941 **Autumn**
Let Us Now Praise Famous Men published by Houghton Mifflin.

October
Begins reviewing films for *Time.*
Moves to Bleeker Street.
Robert Fitzgerald returns to *Time.*

1942 **December, 1942, to September, 1948**
Writes signed column on films for the *Nation.*

1943 **May**
Robert Fitzgerald joins navy.

1945

In the Street, a short, lyrical documentary film, directed and photographed by Helen Levitt, Janice Loeb, James Agee.

Autumn
Begins writing special feature stories for *Time.*
Marries Mia Fritsch.

1946 **November 7**
First daughter, Julia Teresa, is born.
Robert Fitzgerald returns to New York.

1948

Leaves *Time.* Writes, under contract to Huntington Hartford, film scripts based on "The Blue Hotel" and "The Bride Comes to Yellow Sky" by Stephen Crane.
Writes commentary for Helen Levitt's film *The Quiet One.*
World premier of *Knoxville: Summer of 1915* for soprano and orchestra, music by Samuel Barber, words by Agee, with Eleanor Steber singing and Koussevitzsky conducting the Boston Symphony orchestra (recorded, 1950; later recorded with Leontyne Price).

1949 **September 3**
"Comedy's Greatest Era," a study of silent film comedians, published in *Life.*

1950 **May 15**
His second daughter, Andrea Maria, born.

Spring
Robert Fitzgerald sees Agee for the last time.
Louis Kronenberger sees Agee for the last time.

Autumn
Goes to California, to work with John Huston

on a script for *The African Queen,* based on C. S. Forester's novel.

September 18
"Undirectable Director," a portrait of John Huston, is published in *Life.*

1951 **January**
Has first heart attacks, in California.

April
The Morning Watch published by Houghton Mifflin.

1952

Writes script on the life of Lincoln, commissioned by the Ford Foundation for television (*Omnibus,* Robert Saudek, producer).
Whittaker Chambers sees Agee for the last time.

July
"A Mother's Tale" published in *Harper's Bazaar.*

1953

Writes script for *Noa Noa,* based on Paul Gauguin's diary.

1954

Writes script for *The Night of the Hunter,* based on a novel by Davis Grubb.
Father Flye leaves Saint Andrew's after the death of his wife (in January).

September 6
His second son, John Alexander, born.

1955

May 16
Dies of a heart attack while riding in a taxicab in New York City.
Father Flye comes from Wichita to conduct funeral service; Agee is buried in Hillsdale on a farm still owned by Mia.

1957

A Death in the Family published posthumously by McDowell-Obolensky, edited by David McDowell.

1958

A Death in the Family wins Pulitzer-Prize.
Agee on Film, published by McDowell-Obolensky.

1959
Father Flye moves to New York City.

1960
Agee on Film, Volume II, published by McDowell-Obolensky, with foreword by John Huston.
Let Us Now Praise Famous Men, reprinted by Houghton Mifflin, with new preface by Walker Evans.

November 30
All the Way Home, stage adaptation of *A Death in the Family,* opens. Wins Pulitzer Prize and Drama Critics Award.

1961
Letters of James Agee to Father Flye published by George Braziller, Inc., with essay by Robert Phelps.

1963
All the Way Home, screen adaptation of the play and novel appears.

1965
A Way of Seeing, photographs of Spanish Harlem by Helen Levitt, with an essay by James Agee, published by Viking.

1966
Agee, by Peter H. Ohlin, first of four books about Agee, published by Obolensky.
Agee's mother dies.

1967 Fall
Film Heritage publishes special Agee issue.

1968
The Collected Poems of James Agee, edited with an introduction by Robert Fitzgerald, published by Houghton Mifflin.

1969
The Collected Short Prose of James Agee, with "Memoir" by Robert Fitzgerald, published by Houghton Mifflin.

1971
James Agee: A Portrait released by Caedmon records, with Agee speaking "a letter to a friend" and reading from his work (1953), and Father Flye reminiscing and reading from Agee's work.

Second edition of *Letters of James Agee to Father Flye,* with a new preface and previously unpublished letters by Father Flye, published by Houghton Mifflin, introduction by Robert Phelps.

1972 Spring

Harvard Advocate publishes commemorative issue on James Agee.

October

Agee Study Week and Dedication of Memorial Library at Saint Andrew's School in Tennessee.

Notes on Contributors

David Madden was born in Knoxville, Tennessee, in 1933; he grew up there and graduated from the University of Tennessee. Two of his novels, *Cassandra Singing* and *Bijou* (for which he received a Rockefeller Grant in Fiction), were published by Crown, where his editor is David McDowell. LSU Press published a collection of his stories, *The Shadow Knows,* a National Council on the Arts Selection, in 1970. He has also written and edited numerous books of literary criticism and textbooks. Former assistant editor of the *Kenyon Review,* he is currently associate editor of several film and literary journals; he has also published poems and his plays have had numerous productions outside New York.

Father James Harold Flye was a teacher of history at Saint Andrews for almost forty years (1918–1954). He has since then held other posts in Wichita, Kansas, and New York City. Agee's teacher and friend, he edited *Letters of James Agee to Father Flye,* first and second editions.

Robert Saudek was born in Pittsburgh in 1911. He was Agee's roommate at Harvard. A television and film producer, he has won four Peabody and twelve Emmy awards. He produced *Omnibus* on which Agee's series on Lincoln was first presented, and the award-winning series *Profiles in Courage,* based on President John F. Kennedy's book. He is a visiting lecturer in visual studies at Harvard.

Robert Fitzgerald, poet, critic, translator, was born in Geneva, New York, in 1910 and grew up in Springfield, Illinois. One year behind Agee at Harvard, he was a member of the *Harvard Advocate.* He wrote for the *New York Herald Tribune* (1933–1935) and *Time* (1936–1949);

and he taught at Sarah Lawrence (1946–1953) and Princeton (1950–1952); he has been Boylston Professor of Rhetoric at Harvard since 1965. His volumes of poetry are: *Poems* (1935); *A Wreath for the Sea* (1943); *In the Rose of Time* (1956), *Spring Shade* (1971). For his translation of *The Odyssey,* he received the Bollingen Award in 1961. His *Iliad* is to be published in October, 1974. For many years, his permanent residence has been in Perugia, Italy.

David McDowell was born in 1918. From 1931 to 1936, he attended Saint Andrew's, where he first met Agee. He has been an editor for New Directions, Random House, and the *Saturday Evening Post.* He was editor and publisher of *A Death in the Family* and *Agee on Film,* Volumes I and II. Custodian of the James Agee Trust, he is now a senior editor at Crown Publishers. Mr. McDowell is writing a biography of Agee and editing his letters.

Walker Evans was born in 1903 in St. Louis. He began taking photographs in 1928 at the age of twenty-four after returning from studies at the Sorbonne in Paris. He met Agee in Greenwich Village in 1936 and went with him to Alabama to research and take photographs for *Let Us Now Praise Famous Men.* His photographs are collected in three other volumes: *American Photographs* (1938), *Many Are Called* (1966), and *Message from the Interior* (1966). The Museum of Modern Art held a retrospective of his work in 1971. He teaches at Yale.

Louis Kronenberger was born in Cincinnati, Ohio, in 1904. After serving as an editor for Boni & Liveright and Alfred A. Knopf (1926–1935) and as board member of *Fortune* (1936–39), he became drama critic for *Time* (1938–1961). From 1952 until retiring in 1970 he was Professor of Theatre Arts at Brandeis; between 1950 and 1968 he was a visiting professor at Columbia, City College of New York, Harvard, Stanford, and Berkeley; he also gave lectures at Oxford and the Christian Gauss seminars at Princeton. He is a member of the National Institute of Arts and Letters and of the American Academy of Arts and Sciences. Mr. Kronenberger is the author of, among others, *Kings and Desperate Men* (1942), *Company Manners* (1954), *Marlborough's Duchess* (1958), *The Cart and the Horse* (1964), *No Whippings, No Gold Watches* (1970), and *The Extraordinary Mr. Wilkes* (1974). He adapted Jean Anouilh's *Colombe* for Broadway (1954), has edited numerous books including the Burns Mantle *Best Plays* (1953–1961), and has been general editor of the Great Letters series and the Masters of World Literature series.

T. S. Matthews was born in Cincinnati in 1901. Having graduated from Princeton in 1922 and from Oxford in 1924, he worked for the *New Republic* from 1925 to 1929, when he began writing for *Time;* he was managing editor of *Time* from 1943 to 1950; Agee wrote many articles under his editorship. His books include: *To the Gallows I Must Go* (1931), *The Sugar Pill* (1959), *Name and Address* (1960), an autobiography, *O My America!* (1962), and *Great Tom* (1974), a biography of T. S. Eliot. He lives in Suffolk, England.

Dwight Macdonald was born in New York City in 1906. He began corresponding with Agee soon after his graduation from Phillips Exeter Academy in 1924. After graduation from Yale in 1928, he became a staff writer for *Fortune* (1929–1936). He was an editor of *Partisan Review* (1938–1943), editor and publisher of *Politics* (1944–1949), and advisory editor of *Encounter* (1956–1957). He was a movie reviewer for *Esquire* and a staff writer for the *New Yorker* in the fifties and sixties. Among his books are *Henry Wallace, the Man and Myth* (1948), *Memoirs of a Revolutionist* (1957), *Against the American Grain* (1962), and *Dwight Macdonald on Movies* (1969). He is also editor of *Parodies* (1960). A collection of his resent essays, *Discriminations,* is being published this fall by Grossman.

John Huston was born in 1906 in Missouri. Included among the works of this highly individual director, writer, and occasional actor are: *The Maltese Falcon* (1941), his first venture; *Treasure of Sierra Madre* (1947); *The Asphalt Jungle* (1950); *The Red Badge of Courage* (1951); *The African Queen* (1952), the script for which was written predominantly by Agee; *Moby Dick* (1956), an experiment in color, as was *Reflections in a Golden Eye* (1967). Mr. Huston lives in Ireland.

Florence Homolka inspired the following comment by the editor of *Focus on Art: Photography and Notes by Florence Homolka:* "She is a photographer's photographer. An artist in her own right she has moved with quietude and humility through life, and she has photographed extraordinary people under extraordinary conditions—in their homes. Certainly Mrs. Homolka could never have done so had she not received their regard and friendship in return."

Whittaker Chambers was born in 1901 in Philadelphia. He attended Columbia from 1920 to 1922. From 1925 to 1938, he was a member of the Communist party. As book reviewer, writer, and editor at *Time* beginning in 1938, he was a close associate of Agee's. He ran a farm in Westminster, Maryland, from 1938 until his death, July 9, 1961. He was a contributor to *Life's Pictorial History of Western Civilization* (1947), and wrote two autobiographical books, *Witness* (1952) and the posthumously published *Cold Friday* (1964).

Mia Agee was born in Vienna, Austria, and came to the United States in the late thirties. She was a researcher on *Fortune* when she met Agee. The mother of three of Agee's four children, she is currently working at the University of California, San Diego. Her memoir is based on an interview **Gerald Locklin** conducted with her in the winter of 1974. Born in Rochester, New York, in 1941, Mr. Locklin has been teaching literature at California State in Long Beach since 1966; he writes fiction but has published mostly volumes of poetry; two of his essays appear in *Nathanael West: The Cheaters and the Cheated.*

Helen Levitt was born in New York City. With James Agee and Janice Loeb she made *In The Street* (1945), a prize-winning documentary set in the upper East Side of Manhattan. Agee wrote the commentary and dialogue for *The Quiet One* (1948), a feature documentary to which she contributed some camera work; first prize winner at the Venice Film Festival, it is narrated by Gary Merrill. Her photographs have appeared in exhibits at the Museum of Modern Art and the Chicago Institute of Design. Her book of photographs, *A Way of Seeing,* with an essay by Agee, appeared in 1964.